THE
LIFE
BEFORE

THE LIFE BEFORE

HOW OUR PREMORTAL EXISTENCE
AFFECTS OUR MORTAL LIFE

BRENT L. TOP

DESERET
BOOK™

Library of Congress Catalog Card Number: 88-72244

ISBN 0-88494-674-6

Printed in the United States of America   72082-2808B

10   9   8   7   6   5   4   3   2

To my children
Jessica
Justin
Tiffany
Emma Jane

Contents

Preface

A scriptural and theological examination of man's premortal existence and its impact on mortality is, as Elder Neal A. Maxwell has expressed it, "one of the doctrinal roads least traveled by." However fragmentary our veiled mortal knowledge may be, there is something in each of us that seeks for expanding enlightenment regarding our origins. President David O. McKay taught that "everyone is possessed with an irresistible desire to know his relationship with the Infinite." Knowledge of one's literal relationship to God and of one's premortal heavenly associations can, as President McKay continued, "urge him to rise above himself, to control his environment, to master the body and all things physical and live in a higher and more beautiful world."

It is often thought that because a veil is drawn and we cannot remember, there must not be very much known about that spiritual realm. Some also seem to regard it as a topic that is "off limits." Yet there are many things that we naturally wonder about concerning that former abode. The expansive understanding that we once possessed has since been muted, leaving only intimations, suppositions, and partially answered questions. To attempt to answer all of the questions would be impossible, since the Lord, in his infinite wisdom, has withheld much regarding our premortal home. However, the scriptures and, particularly, the inspired writings and utterances of latter-day prophets have parted the veil just enough to provide impelling insights. The Brethren have written or spoken much more on this subject than most of us imagine. The scriptures, likewise, speak to us in sometimes indirect ways to teach us about our life before mortality. The purpose of this book is certainly not to speculate or theorize about things hidden from our view but rather to compile and organize those scriptural and seeric statements that can inform and inspire, and to draw reasonable conclusions therefrom. The more we can learn about the life before, the more we will be motivated to live worthy to return to the presence of our Eternal Father.

There will remain many unanswered questions. The veil will yet be drawn. It is my hope, however, that this book will help to answer some questions and, more important, to stimulate your thinking—for as you ponder and study, more questions will arise, followed by greater spiritual insight. "Knowledge is of no value unless used," said President Spencer W. Kimball. That is the objective of this book—to provide information that will enlighten the mind and prepare the heart for the inspiration that can change our lives and buoy us up spiritually as we pass through this second estate.

Acknowledgments

Several people have helped to shape the words and ideas of this book. I extend to each of them my appreciation for their important input. Thomas F. Olmstead, coordinator for the Church Educational System in the Richmond, Virginia, area, first encouraged me to seriously pursue this project. I appreciate the research ideas he shared with me. I also appreciate my former colleagues of the Church Educational System, U. S. Northeast Area, who served as sounding boards for many of my ideas.

Several of my colleagues from the BYU religion faculty also helped in a variety of ways with this project. I appreciate the input of ideas, editorial suggestions, and critical feedback that I received from Robert L. Millet, Stephen E. Robinson, Kent P. Jackson, Joseph F. McConkie, and Art Bailey. I am especially grateful for the "extra-mile" service of my colleague, friend, and mentor, Larry E. Dahl, who continually encouraged me in my research and writing. He unselfishly shared not only much of his own research but also his time in reviewing the manuscript and offering valuable suggestions. My association with all of my colleagues of the BYU religion faculty has influenced this work indirectly. I am daily touched by their enormous collective and individual knowledge of and love for the gospel, and by their deep commitment to religious education and gospel scholarship.

I am deeply grateful for my four children and for the contribution they have unknowingly made to this book.

Their love, their character, and their questions have stimulated my desire for research on this subject. While carefully observing them, I have gained many insights about our premortal existence. In them I can see that, in a spiritually significant way, as Tiffany said, their "insides are older than their outsides."

Most important, I extend my love and appreciation to my wife, Wendy, for her assistance in this work. She has unwearyingly reviewed, edited, and improved the manuscript. She not only has given significant editorial service but also has influenced my ideas with her own inspired insights. I deeply needed and profoundly felt her support and encouragement. With this project, as with other more eternally important endeavors we share, she has been an inspiration in my life.

Man's Search for His Spiritual Roots

Several years ago, Alex Haley captivated the American public with his epic novel, *Roots*, and its subsequent television miniseries. That monumental work aroused a new fascination with genealogies and family histories. Soon many became fervently involved in tracing family "roots" and in delving into the annals of ancestors. Like Haley, others felt that discovering their own biological and cultural heritage would lead them to greater understanding of their own identity. It is undeniably true that our roots help shape the trunk, branches, and limbs that make up not only ourselves and our posterity but also, ultimately, all of mankind.

Just as the discovery of our earthly genealogy, enhanced by familial and cultural history, can guide us to a greater understanding of our temporal selves, perhaps even greater insight into the eternal nature and destiny of man emerges from a search for our spiritual roots or eternal lineage. In virtually all mankind there is some sort of innate yearning to know what was before this life and how it affects man in his earthly sojourn. Eliza R. Snow, in the familiar hymn "O My Father," expressed this yearning for a knowledge of spiritual roots:

> For a wise and glorious purpose
> Thou hast placed me here on earth
> And withheld the recollection
> Of my former friends and birth;
> Yet ofttimes a secret something
> Whispered, "You're a stranger here,"
> And I felt that I had wandered
> From a more exalted sphere.[1]

This feeling or intimation of a former existence, described by Eliza R. Snow as a "secret something," is not unique to Latter-day Saints. Several surveys conducted during the last three decades among peoples from many countries in the Western world—countries whose cultures and religions generally reject the notion of a premortal life of man—found substantial numbers of the population who felt strongly that there was a life or existence before their present life on earth.[2] With regard to the ample sentiment among men and women of all cultures, religions, and backgrounds for a premortal existence of man, Erik Erikson, a noted psychoanalyst, observed, "And let us face it: 'deep down' nobody in his right mind can visualize his own existence without assuming that he has always lived and will live hereafter; and the religious world-views of old only endowed this psychological instinct with images which could be shared, transmitted, and ritualized."[3]

This feeling or sense of the premortal existence and immortality of the soul, described by Erikson as a "psychological instinct," surfaces in many sources. Man's yearning to know his spiritual roots and to understand more fully the meaning of his premortal life threads through the writings and beliefs of people throughout all ages and across diverse cultures, religions, and philosophies.

Anthropologists have reported a strong belief in the immortality of the soul of man and in the concept of "rebirth" among age-old African folk religions.[4] *Roots* offered us a sample of these ancient African beliefs. The main character, Kunta Kinte, learns of the premortal existence and the life beyond mortality from his father, Omoro, upon the death of his beloved grandmother. "He said that three groups of people lived in every village," explains Haley. "First were those you could see—walking around, eating, sleeping, and working. Second were the ancestors, whom Grandma Yaisa had now joined. 'And the third people—who are they?' asked Kunta. 'The third people,' said Omoro, 'are those waiting to be born.' "[5]

The age-old African folk beliefs depicted by Haley are also evident in the writings of Chinua Achebe, a Nigerian novelist. Achebe, like other West African writers, has drawn upon the folk stories, legends, and spiritual beliefs of his people in the development of his literary works. Some of this folklore described by Achebe has intriguing references to a life before mortality. In African tradition, Achebe says, "the idea of the child as a messenger is certainly prevalent." There are many African tribal stories "about how children come from the world over there into the world of men. . . . The child comes from somewhere else . . . [and] there is a constant coming or going between us and the world of the ancestors. . . . Then it's the child who can tell you about that world since its coming from there—it's not the old man who's *going* there but the child who's *coming* from there."[6]

When the Romans conquered the Celts, they discovered a people with strong beliefs in the immortality of the spirit of man. Historian Alfred Nutt reported that these ancient peoples of the British Isles held definite religious views regarding a premortal existence of man and the concept of rebirth from a previous life.[7] Such folklore is exemplified in this statement from the Scottish poet Fiona Macleod: "I think the soul knows. I think the soul remembers. I think that intuition is divine and unshakeable. We have travelled a long way, and forgotten much. The secret road of the soul is a long road."[8]

While other cultures and civilizations have shared many of these beliefs, each with its own unique adaptations, perhaps the most widely known cultural acceptance of the immortality and previous existence of man's soul is found in the Eastern religions, and this acceptance is embodied in the doctrine of reincarnation. Though not generally accepted in Western culture, the concept of reincarnation has gained much publicity in recent times with considerable media attention focused on prominent figures from the entertainment world who have embraced a belief in reincarnation and the immortality of the soul. Even modern psychologists have exerted considerable time and effort in the study of "past lives" and beliefs about reincarnation. Despite the recent public interest in this idea, the concept is not new and its roots can be traced to ancient Eastern religious thought. While Latter-day Saints reject the doctrine of reincarnation as taught in Hinduism, Buddhism, and other religions, our theology shares with it many important principles, such as the immortality and preexistence of the spirit and the doctrine of restoration. Thus, despite theological differences, a commonality exists that sheds light on the idea of a premortal existence.

The ancient Greeks accepted the notions of a premortal state for man and the immortality of the spirit. Famous Greek writers and philosophers such as Plato, Cicero, and Seneca wrote extensively concerning this idea. Plato, responding to Socrates in his famous dialogue *Phaedo*, remarks, "Your favourite doctrine, Socrates, that knowledge is simply recollection, if true, also necessarily implies a previous time in which we have learned that which we now recollect. But this would be impossible unless our soul had been in some place before existing in the form of man; here then is another proof of the soul's immortality."[9]

In addition to the Greek philosophers, Philo of Alexandria, the Jewish theologian who was a contemporary of the early Apostles of Jesus, also spoke of a premortal existence of man. David Winston, a noted expert in Greek and early Jewish literature, reported some interesting similarities between LDS views on the premortal existence and Greek and Jewish writings. "Analogous doctrines may be found in ancient Greek and Jewish literature, though with subtle and important variations. We shall find, for example, that the notions of preexistence, the creation of the world out of primordial matter, and the placing of human life on earth for moral testing, are in one form or another common to Mormonism and the Hellenic and Jewish traditions. The eternal generation of spirits by God may be partially paralleled in Greek and Jewish-Hellenistic writings, though not in rabbinic literature."[10]

Hugh Nibley has done considerable research in this area and has given numerous examples from apocryphal and other writings, including those from Qumran, Nag Hammadi, and the Mandaeans, that speak not only of a premortal existence of man but also of a unique relationship to a Heavenly Father.[11] With increasing discoveries of such scrolls and documents of ancient origin, evidence has come to light more frequently that these early civilizations believed that man himself had a premortal life. Truman G. Madsen noted that one scholar now estimates that there are "well over eight hundred references to the premortal existence of mankind in Jewish and Christian source materials."[12]

As we study the references to these beliefs in a previous existence of man across the many cultures and religions of the world, one important question arises: How can there be so many similarities in belief concerning a previous existence and immortality and yet such diversity among those beliefs? It is logical to assume that each of these cultures and religions was exposed to some of the truth, as evidenced in their basic belief in a previous existence, but what accounts for those teachings that are far from the truth? The First Presidency issued an official statement in 1978 that helps to account not only for the similarities but also for the differences in belief among the great religions and philosophies of the world:

> Based upon ancient and modern revelation, The Church of Jesus Christ of Latter-day Saints gladly teaches and declares the Christian doctrine that all men and women are brothers and sisters, not only by blood relationship from common mortal progenitors, but also as literal spirit children of an Eternal Father.
>
> The great religious leaders of the world such as Mohammed, Confucius, and the Reformers, as well as philosophers including Socrates, Plato, and others, received a portion of God's light. Moral truths were given to them by God to enlighten whole nations and to bring a higher level of understanding to individuals. . . .
>
> Consistent with these truths, we believe that God has given and will give to all people sufficient knowledge to help them on their way to eternal salvation, either in this life or in the life to come.[13]

Not only has the Lord revealed portions of the truth regarding the origins of man to great religious leaders and philosophers in an effort to lift them and their people to a nobler, more purposeful existence, and thereby to lead them to the fulness of the gospel, but he has also inspired other thoughtful and sensitive individuals in many other walks of life and in many lands to "a higher level of understanding." This higher level of understanding is reflected in the personal musings of searching individuals in literature, philosophy, psychology, and other disciplines.

Most Latter-day Saints are familiar with the famous lines of William Wordsworth:

> Our birth is but a sleep and a forgetting:
> The Soul that rises with us, our life's Star,
> Hath had elsewhere its setting,
> And cometh from afar:
> Not in entire forgetfulness,

> And not in utter nakedness,
> But trailing clouds of glory do we come
> From God, who is our home:
> Heaven lies about us in our infancy!

Not as familiar as these beautiful lines are Wordsworth's personal comments concerning the ideas that influenced him to write "Ode: Intimations of Immortality from Recollections of Early Childhood." He wrote of childhood memories and images which he described as the "presumptive evidence of a prior state of existence." He further commented:

> I think it right to protest against a conclusion, which has given pain to some good and pious persons, that I meant to inculcate such a belief. It is far too shadowy a notion to be recommended to faith, as more than an element in our instincts of immortality. But let us bear in mind that, though the idea is not advanced in revelation, there is nothing there to contradict it, and the fall of Man presents an analogy in its favour. Accordingly, a preexistent state has entered into the popular creeds of many nations; and, among all persons acquainted with classic literature, is known as an ingredient in Platonic philosophy. . . . Having to wield some of its elements when I was impelled to write this poem on the "Immortality of the Soul," I took hold of the notion of preexistence as having sufficient foundation in humanity for authorizing me to make for my purpose the best use of it I could as a poet.[14]

Wordsworth is not alone among literary figures in writing about this subject. Alfred, Lord Tennyson, also wrote with wonder about the possibility of former worlds and premortal relationships:

> . . . We say "All this hath been before,
> All this hath been, I know not when or where."
> So, friend, when first I looked upon your face,
> Our thought gave answer, each to each, so true,
> Opposed mirrors each reflecting each—
> Altho' I knew not in what time or place,
> Methought that I had often met with you,
> And lived in each other's mind and speech.[15]

A hundred years or so before either Wordsworth or Tennyson penned their lines, the poet Henry Vaughn wrote of a "celestial" home and of a new home "appointed for my second race." Such a description certainly is an intriguing parallel to the common LDS terminology for mortality as the "second estate."

> Happy those early days, when I
> Shin'd in my Angel-Infancy!
> Before I understood this place
> Appointed for my second race,
> Or taught my soul to fancy aught
> But a white celestial thought:
> When yet I had not walk'd above
> A mile or two from my first Love,
> And looking back—at that short space—
> Could see a glimpse of His bright face.[16]

The works of Thomas Traherne came to light only in this century, but he also made several references to man's immortal spirit and celestial lineage. In the mid-seventeenth century his works were viewed as radical at best and heretical at worst. The prevailing religious thought of his day was of the innate sinfulness and fallen state of man. Traherne, however, alluded to a more pure spirit of man which had its origins in a heavenly home. His strong belief in man's celestial roots and in his inherent goodness appears in Traherne's own meditations as well as his poetic works. "Will you see the infancy of this sublime and celestial greatness?" mused Traherne. "Those pure and virgin apprehensions I had in my infancy, and that divine light wherewith I was born. . . . I was a little stranger which at my entrance into the world was saluted and surrounded with innumerable joys. My knowledge was divine; I knew by intuition those things which since my apostasy I collected again by highest reason."[17]

In his poetry, Traherne also used terms and phrases that to Latter-day Saints may hint that he had an intimation of a previous spiritual existence. While we must be careful not to read too much into his writings or to interpret his poems to meet our own preconceived notions or doctrinal objectives, it is fascinating to look at those terms and lines and to ponder what he must have felt and believed. In his poem, "The Preparative," he describes his birth with beautiful imagery and uses the term "intelligence," which certainly has significance in light of modern revelation:

> Before my Tongue or Cheeks were to me shewn,
>   Before I knew my Hands were mine,
> Or that my Sinews did my Members joyn,
>   When neither Nostril, Foot, or Ear,
> As yet was seen or felt, or did appear;
>   I was within
> A House I knew not, newly clothed with Skin.
>
> Then was my Soul my only All to me.
>   A Living Endless Ey,
>   Just bounded with the Skie
> Whose Power, whose Act, whose Essence was to see.
>   I was an inward Sphere of Light,
>   Or an Interminable Orb of Sight,
>   An Endless and a Living Day,
> A vital Sun that round about did ray
>   All Life, all Sence,
> A Naked Simple Pure Intelligence.[18]

In two other poems, Traherne returns to the theme. In "The Rapture," he writes, "From God above Being sent, the Heavens me enflame. . . . O how divine Am I!" In "The Salutation," he asks, "Where have ye been? Behind what curtain were ye from me hid so long?" Finally, in his work entitled "Wonder," Traherne writes:

> How like an Angel came I down!
>   How bright are all things here!
> When first among his Works I did appear
>   O how their Glory me did crown?
> The World resembled his Eternitie.[19]

In his novel *Demian*, Herman Hesse, the eminent German novelist, also spoke of the spirit of man. The novel is about a young boy's search for his own true identity. In that search, Hesse uses several images of a rebirth or reawakening from some previous knowledge or existence. In the prologue to *Demian*, Hesse writes:

> I cannot tell my story without reaching a long way back. If it were possible I would reach back farther still—into the very first years of my childhood, and beyond them into distant ancestral past. . . .
>
> . . . Every man is more than just himself; he also represents the unique, the very special and always significant and remarkable point at which the world's phenomena intersect. . . . That is why every man's story is important, eternal, sacred. . . . In each individual the spirit has become flesh. . . .
>
> Each man's life represents a road toward himself, an attempt at such a road, the intimation of a path. No man has ever been entirely and completely himself. . . . Each man carries the vestiges of his birth—the slime and eggshells of his primeval past—with him to the end of his days. . . . We all share the same origin; . . . all of us come in at the same door.[20]

Marcel Proust, who was perhaps the most influential of modern French novelists, was another author who seems to have given profound thought to the idea of a premortal life. Writes Proust, "Everything in our life happens as though we entered upon it with a load of obligations contracted in a previous existence . . . obligations whose sanction is not of this present life, [which] seem to belong to a different world, founded on kindness, scruples, sacrifice, a world entirely different from this one, a world whence we emerge to be born on this earth, before returning thither."[21]

In addition to poets Wordsworth, Vaughn, Traherne, and Tennyson, and novelists Hesse and Proust, numerous other writers not only of literature but also of philosophy and psychology have advocated their ideas on the immortality of man's soul.[22] In fact, many of the prevailing teachings in modern psychology refer to man's "larger consciousness" as a collection of personality traits and attitudes that the soul or mind of man has acquired from previous experience. Dr. M. Scott Peck, a noted psychiatrist and author, attempted to explain this enigma in his thoughtful book, *The Road Less Traveled.*

> How did I know this which I did not know? Among the possible explanations, one is that of Jung's theory of the "collective unconscious," in which we inherit the wisdom of the experience of our ancestors without ourselves having the personal experience. While this kind of knowledge may seem bizarre to the scientific mind, strangely enough its existence is recognized in our common everyday language. Take the word "recognize" itself. . . . The word says we "re-know" the concept, as if we knew it once upon a time, forgot it, but then recognized it as an old friend. It is as if all knowledge and all wisdom were contained in our minds, and when we learn "something new" we are actually only discovering something that existed in our self all along.[23]

While this psychological phenomenon, puzzled over by great thinkers such as Carl Jung and Sigmund Freud, may be difficult to accept or understand without a belief in the literal existence of the spirit of man prior to his birth, it rings true to those who accept the immortality of the soul. The "larger consciousness" or "larger self" spoken of by the noted English scientist Sir Oliver Lodge is readily identified as the spirit of man which was schooled and enlarged upon in a premortal realm and subsequently influences the psychological and intellectual traits of the mortal person. Lodge observed, "We living men and women, while associated with this mortal organism, are ignorant of whatever experience our larger selves may have gone through in the past—yet when we wake out of this present materialized condition, we may gradually realize . . . the wide range of knowledge which that larger entity must have accumulated since its intelligence and memory began."[24] This psychological theory merges with theological fact in the words of Elder Neal A. Maxwell: "The reality of premortality responds to puzzlings which suggest we are strangers here. It is a curative for the yearnings expressed in music and poetry and literature. . . . Thus when we now say 'I know,' that realization is rediscovery; we are actually saying 'I know—again!' From long experience, His sheep know His voice and His doctrine."[25]

Thus we see that through years of "scientific" inquiry into the human mind, psychologists and psychiatrists have theorized what thoughtful poets and authors have intimated, what philosophers have philosophized, and what ancient civilizations have faithfully believed and celebrated in one form or another: man has spiritual roots which reach far back beyond this existence.

In addition to all of the supposing of poets and philosophers and doctors and religious leaders throughout the centuries, there is something deep within each of us individually, which, if heeded, whispers, "You're a stranger here." Often we need no source outside ourselves to tell us what we already feel, as was so eloquently stated by this early Church leader, H. W. Naisbitt.

> There is something in every man and in every woman which savors of the divine, in all the circumstances of life there is a reaching out after something which is beyond the grasp; there is a soaring of the spirit, a seeking after something to which the present surrounding gave no clue. Man feels that he is. He not only feels that he is, but thousands and millions of the human family have an inkling of the great fact that they have been, and millions and millions more have an inkling of the other great fact that when they leave this stage of existence they will continue to be. And it is the realization of such things which establishes the idea outside of any other special revelation that our origin is divine as well as human.[26]

Fortunately, though we may need no special revelation to tell us we had a life before, such revelation exists. Plentiful enough in scripture and in prophetic teachings, these revelatory insights not only confirm our intimations but also paint a clear and understandable picture of just who we are, where we came from, and why we are here. Without this modern revelation we could only guess at what it all means, but with it the scriptures unveil a meaning hidden to the rest of the world—the premortal heavens are no longer a mystery.

Notes

1. Eliza R. Snow, "O My Father," *Hymns*, no. 292.

2. Sylvia Cranston and Carey Williams, *Reincarnation: A New Horizon in Science, Religion and Society* (New York: Julian Press, 1984), pp. 12–15.

3. Eric Erikson, *Gandhi's Truth* (New York: Norton, 1969), pp. 35–36.

4. Cranston and Williams, *Reincarnation*, pp. 164–166. (References are given to several other cultures with similar beliefs, i.e., Australian aborigines, Polynesians, native American Indians. For a complete description of these cultural religious beliefs regarding the immortality of man's soul, see pages 166–179.)

5. Alex Haley, *Roots* (New York: Doubleday, 1976), p. 18.

6. Jonathan Cott, "Chinua Achebe: At The Crossroads— An Interview with the Nigerian Writer," *Parabola—Myth and the Quest for Meaning*, vol. 6 no. 2, pp. 28–39.

7. Alfred Nutt, *The Voyage of Bran*, "The Celtic Doctrine of Rebirth" edited by Kuno Meyer vol. II (London: published by David Nutt, 1895–1897), chapters xiv and xv, pp. 38–123.

8. Fiona Macleod, as quoted in Cranston and Williams, *Reincarnation*, pp. 163–164.

9. Plato, "Phaedo," *The Portable Plato*, translated by Benjamin Jowett, edited with commentary by Scott Buchanan (New York: Viking Press, 1948), p. 213; see pp. 191–278.

10. David Winston, "Preexistence in Hellenic, Judaic and Mormon Sources," chapter 2 in *Reflections on Mormonism*, edited by Truman G. Madsen (Provo, Utah: Religious Studies Center, Brigham Young University, 1978), pp. 14–15; see pp. 14–35.

11. Hugh Nibley, *Old Testament and Related Studies*, vol. 1 of *The Collected Works of Hugh Nibley* edited by John W. Welch, Gary

P. Gillum, Don E. Norton (Salt Lake City: Deseret Book Co. and The Foundation for Ancient Research and Mormon Studies, 1986), pp. 171–214. For additional source material on the premortal life in early Christian writings, see Hugh Nibley, *The World and the Prophets* (Salt Lake City: Deseret Book Co., 1974), pp. 205ff.

12. Truman G. Madsen, in *Reflections on Mormonism*, p. 13.

13. First Presidency statement, February 15, 1978, as quoted in the preface to *The Expanding Church*, Spencer J. Palmer (Salt Lake City: Deseret Book Co., 1978).

14. William Wordsworth, "Ode: Intimations of Immortality from Recollections of Early Childhood," *English Romantic Poetry and Prose*, edited with essays and notes by Alfred Noyes (New York: Oxford University Press, 1956), pp. 327–328.

15. Alfred, Lord Tennyson, "Early Sonnet," *Poems of Tennyson* (London: Oxford University Press, 1929), pp. 108–109.

16. Henry Vaughn, "The Retreat," *The Complete Poetry of Henry Vaughn*, edited by French Fogle (New York: New York University Press, 1965), p. 169.

17. Thomas Traherne, *The Poetical Works of Thomas Traherne*, edited with preface and notes by Gladys I. Wade (London: P.J. and A.E. Dobell, 1932), p. xxvi.

18. Thomas Traherne, "The Preparative," *The Poetical Works of Thomas Traherne*, pp. 11–12; italics added.

19. Thomas Traherne, *The Poetical Works of Thomas Traherne*: "The Rapture," p. 17; "The Salutation," p. 3; "Wonder," p. 5.

20. Hermann Hesse, *Demian*, translated by Michael Roloff and Michael Lebeck (New York: Bantam Books, 1965), pp. 3–4.

21. Marcel Proust, in Gabriel Marcel, *Homo Viator* (New York: Harper and Row, 1963), p. 8, as quoted by Elder Neal A. Maxwell in Conference Report, October 1985, p. 19.

22. Gary Ellsworth, "Trailing Clouds of Glory—Poets and Philosophers Examine the Preexistence," *Ensign*, October 1974, pp. 49–51.

23. M. Scott Peck, M.D., *The Road Less Traveled* (New York: Touchstone Books, Simon and Schuster, 1978), p. 252.

24. Sir Oliver Lodge, *Science and Immortality* (New York: Moffat, Yard and Co., 1910), p. 184.

25. Neal A. Maxwell, in Conference Report, October 1985, p. 22.

26. H. W. Naisbitt, in *Journal of Discourses*, 21:104.

2

Theological Glimpses of Man's Premortal Existence

Despite the many inspired references to a pre-earth life in cultures, religions, literature, and intellectual thought around the world, most of modern Christianity rejects such a notion. This, however, has not always been the case. In addition to the examples of insight that have already been cited, there are numerous theological "glimpses" into man's spiritual origins. These theological references come from a variety of sources, including the writings of the early Christian fathers and theologians as well as more recently discovered ancient manuscripts such as those from Qumran, Nag Hammadi, and elsewhere. These early writings on the premortal existence of man, though often viewed by conventional Christianity as speculative or apocryphal, take on even greater significance when viewed in light of biblical references to the doctrine. And finally, through modern revelation, inspired latter-day prophets have lifted the doctrine further out of ambiguity and obscurity, leaving no doubt as to its truthfulness.

Early Christian Theologians and
the Doctrine of Preexistence

There is considerable evidence which suggests that the doctrine of a premortal existence was common in the early Church and was discussed openly by theologians such as Pierus and John of Jerusalem into the sixth century A.D. Some of these early Christians believed strongly that much of our earthly experience could be understood only in terms of premortal agreements and of a plan established before the foundation of the world. One such early Christian writer sharing this view was Papias. Speaking of the "Elders," he wrote, "To some of them, that is, those angels who had been faithful to God in former times, he gave supervision over the governments of the earth, trusting or commissioning them to rule well. . . . And nothing has occurred [since] to put an end to their order."[1]

In addition to Papias, other prominent early Christian theologians such as Justin the Martyr and Clement of Alexandria also made references to a premortal plan that was presented to the "first angels." Clement, commenting on the scriptural passage in Jeremiah in which the Lord states that he knew Jeremiah before birth, generalized the doctrine as having universal application. He wrote that "the Logos is not to be despised as something new, for even in Jeremiah the Lord says, 'Say not "I am too young," for before I formed thee in the womb I knew thee, and before thou camest forth from thy mother I sanctified thee.' It is possible that in speaking these things the prophet is referring to us, as being known to God as faithful before the foundation of the world."[2]

St. Augustine, to a lesser degree, also taught of a premortal state of man. He spoke of the mind and the reasoning ability of man as being immortal and eternal. Could it be that he was indeed speaking of man's spirit when he referred to the eternal mind of man in his work "On the Immortality of the Soul"? Augustine wrote:

> If science exists anywhere, and cannot exist except in that which lives; and if it is eternal, and nothing in which an eternal thing exists can be non-eternal; then that in which science exists lives eternally. Further, if science cannot exist except in that which lives . . . then science is in the mind of man. Science is eternal. For what exists and is unchangeable must be eternal.
>
> When we reason it is the mind that reasons. For only he who thinks reasons. Neither does the body think nor does the mind receive help of the body in thinking. For what is thought is thus eternal, and nothing pertaining to the body is thus eternal. All that the mind knows, moreover, it contains within itself. Therefore the human mind always lives.[3]

Another common theme relating to the premortal existence of man was that of man's innate yearning to return to a heavenly home. This idea was articulated by the early Christian writer, Tertullian. He maintained that the Christian "is a pilgrim in a strange land, among enemies: his is *another race, another dwelling,* another hope, another grace, another dignity."[4] This statement, among others of the early Christian fathers, has caused Hugh Nibley to pose these pertinent questions and make this important conclusion:

> But how can we be out of our element here if this [mortality] is the only element we have ever known? Here we are lost and ill at ease. Lost from what? The theory of the later fathers is that man has an irresistible urge to get to heaven because he was created for the express purpose of filling the gap left in heaven by the fall of the angels. But the same fathers who maintain this doctrine also hold that the vast majority of spirits thus created will never see heaven—a strange inconsistency indeed. The early Christians thought of the yearnings of the soul for heaven specifically as an urge to return to a familiar home.[5]

No other early Christian theologian and scholar spoke more extensively or more explicitly regarding man's premortal existence and its impact on mortality than Origen of Alexandria. His writings of the third century caused a furor among leaders of the early Church after his death. It was his belief that the many differences seen among men on earth could be traced back to the differences in rank and glory of the premortal angels. Without such a belief in a premortal existence, he maintained, it would not be possible to view God as "no respecter of persons," but rather God would seem arbitrary, cruel, and unjust. Origen believed that the differences among men on earth, as with the "angels," were based on merit. Just as there would be a judgment at the end of man's earth life, Origen believed that some sort of judgment had already taken place before we came here which was based on work done in a premortal state. In applying this principle to Jacob's being preferred over Esau, Origen wrote, "We believe that he was even then chosen by God because of merits acquired before this life."[6]

Despite concurring beliefs held by others, Origen's teachings were zealously attacked by his opponents and criticized as unscriptural, too speculative, and having too much the element of Greek thought. Origen had his supporters as well, but in the end the critics got their way, and the proponents of a premortal life of man and the immortality of the soul were censured. In A.D. 543, the Roman emperor, Justinian, coerced the pope to convene a council to reject the teachings of Origen. In an edict known as the Anathemas Against Origen, the teachings of Origen, including his inspired writings on the premortal life of man, were declared heresy in the Church. From this date on, the doctrine of man's premortal state and relationship to God was viewed as heretical and unfounded in scripture of early Christian religious thought. Today conventional Christianity vehemently rejects the notion of a premortal existence but fails to remember that the doctrine was widely taught and accepted prior to the Council of A.D. 543. Even today, some modern Christian scholars view this council and its repudiation of Origen's teachings with a degree of regret and skepticism. One current Christian scholar has written:

> While it is true that a Council of Constantinople in the sixth century A.D. pronounced belief in the preexistence of the soul to be heretical, an examination of the scriptures strongly suggests that the doctrine of rebirth was generally accepted in those days and that Our Lord himself believed it. Whether this be the case or not, the student of the Christian doctrine may well ask whether a decision made by a group of men in the sixth century should be regarded as binding today. . . .
>
> In any case, heresy thus condemned so long ago need not be regarded today as of major importance. Truth matters a great deal more and a condemned heresy may turn out to be a truth, as happened, for example, when a local church of Rome condemned Galileo's heliocentric doctrine and forced him to recant. Galileo was right and the church in question was wrong. It is therefore quite legitimate for both clergy and laity of the Christian faith to preach and believe in [a] preexistence.[7]

Even after the doctrine of premortal existence had disappeared from the accepted teachings of the Church, it periodically resurfaced in the writings of thoughtful and inspired Christian theologians. One such theologian was Jacob Boehme, the seventeenth-century religious leader and philosopher. During the Reformation, Boehme wrote concerning man's soul: "As the eye of man reaches the stars where it had its primitive origin, so the soul penetrates and sees even within the divine state of being wherein he lives."[8]

These theological glimpses of the premortal life of man as set forth in the writings and teachings of the early Christian fathers have faded through the years until now the doctrine is rejected by the churches who once embraced it. Yet these glimpses are not isolated, apostate teachings but can be substantiated with still other theological references to man's premortal state and his relationship to God.

Early Christian and Jewish Writings
on the Preexistence

When the Prophet Joseph Smith was involved in the work of translating the Old Testament, he questioned the Lord concerning the role and value of the Apocrypha. In answer to his questions, the Lord revealed to him what is now Doctrine and Covenants section 91, which gave some important guidelines concerning apocryphal writings. "There are many things contained therein that are true, and it is mostly translated correctly; There are many things contained therein that are not true, which are interpolations by the hands of men. . . . Therefore, whoso readeth it, let him understand, for the Spirit manifesteth truth; And whoso is enlightened by the Spirit shall obtain benefit therefrom." (D&C 91:1–2, 4–5.)

Not only was this a valuable revelation for guiding Joseph in his translation of the scriptures in 1833 but also it is valuable to us today in gleaning truths from the Apocrypha and numerous other apocryphal writings that have come to light in recent times. Many of these ancient documents contain important glimpses of man's premortal origins.

Josephus, the Jewish historian, wrote of the Essenes as a Jewish sect who believed in the immortal soul of man. He wrote that these Essenes taught that the soul of man was indestructible and was imprisoned, temporarily, in a mortal body. In addition to immortality and premortal existence, the Essenes also ascribed divinity to the soul of man.[9] Josephus's early description of Essene doctrine has taken on greater validity in light of the discovery of the Dead Sea Scrolls at Qumran. The Dead Sea Scrolls of the Essenes and other significant finds have now given strong, concurring evidence of a belief in a premortal existence among these early contemporaries of Christ and the Apostles.

There are other evidences that there was a belief in a premortal existence of man among Jewish sects in the Christian era. Commenting on the phrase "all souls are prepared . . .

before the foundation of the world," which is found in the apocryphal text, the Book of Enoch, R. H. Charles, the eminent expert on the Apocrypha and Pseudepigrapha, noted that "the doctrine of the preexistence of the soul . . . became a prevailing dogma of later Judaism. . . . All souls which were to enter human bodies existed before the creation of the world in the Garden of Eden. . . . According to *Bereshith rabba*, c. 8, God takes counsel with the souls of the righteous before He creates the earth."[10]

In several of his works Hugh Nibley has given us numerous examples from the writings of these apocryphal scrolls and libraries which refer to man's premortal existence with God. In the Gospel of Philip we learn that man is literally a child of God. In the Apocryphon of James we read that the Lord told the Apostles, "They will ask you where you are going." And He told them to answer, "To the place from which I came. I return to that place." "When they ask you who you are," it continues, "say 'I am a son and I come from the Father.' And when they ask you what sort of son and from what father, answer, 'From the preexistent Father and I am a son of the Preexistence.'" A psalm on these ancient scrolls states, "The spirit existed before the flesh."[11]

The Gospel of Thomas refers to the elect of God as those who find the kingdom of heaven because they came from it in the first place. The Psalm of Thomas speaks of the return to a heavenly home. "I came from the house of my Father in a far land, and I shall mount up until I return to that land of the pure."[12] Other scrolls speak of man as being older than the world and a child of an earlier spiritual birth or creation.

After citing numerous references to man's premortal life and his divine relationship to God, Nibley concluded that, to the writers of these early Christian and Jewish texts, "Man's premortal existence was an illustrious one. There are descriptions of the glory we enjoyed before we came here."[13]

Joseph Fielding McConkie also has identified references in these ancient texts not only to the immortality of man's soul but also to foreordinations and premortal heavenly councils. While there is still debate among the scholars concerning the authorship and inspiration of many of these ancient writings, one text in particular displays unique insight and understanding. It is found in the Acts of Thomas and is known as the Syriac Hymn of the Pearl. McConkie has given us this summation of this ancient apocryphal yet inspired glimpse of the doctrine of premortal life:

> This is an allegory of a king's son who is required to leave his father's kingdom, where he enjoyed great wealth, to obtain a pearl. The pearl, quite obviously, is a symbol of his own soul. His parents see that he is properly provisioned for his journey. Before leaving their presence he is required to surrender his splendid robe. This robe, or garment of light, we are told, had been woven to the measure of his stature. He also enters into a covenant with them to obtain the pearl and return that he might once again enjoy their presence and wear his splendid robe. The covenant is written upon his heart.
>
> Though the way is hazardous and difficult, an intimate friend referred to as "an (anointed one)" warns him of the dangers that beset him. Notwithstanding all this he soon forgets his identity as a king's son and his mission to obtain the pearl. At this point a council is held; it is attended by his father, his mother, his brother (the crown prince), and many other great and mighty ones. They determine to send him a letter imploring him to awake and remember who he is and what king he serves. He is encouraged to remember his splendid robe and to so conduct himself that his name might be written in the book of heroes, and that with his brother he may be an heir to his father's kingdom.
>
> Thus reminded, he commences again his efforts to obtain the pearl, which he must wrestle from a terrible serpent. This he is able to do only by naming his father's name, that of his brother, and that of his mother. Having obtained the pearl he flees Egypt, sheds his dirty and unclean garments, and is further guided by the letter. At this point he is greeted by messengers from his parents, who clothe him once more in his royal robe, and he returns as an heir to his father's kingdom.[14]

The great value of these ancient apocryphal texts is that they verify that the doctrine of a premortal existence was common among the early Christians as well as among ancient Jewish sects. By themselves certainly they do not prove man's premortal existence or serve as the foundation for LDS beliefs, but rather they provide additional evidence of the validity of the doctrine when coupled with scriptural teachings. As Joseph Fielding McConkie concluded after enumerating and describing several of these glimpses in the ancient Jewish and Christian texts, "The doctrines of premortal existence, heavenly councils, and foreordinations were all a part of the theology of the ancient Saints and as such are a necessary part of the promised restoration of all things. Not found in the theology of the rest of the so-called Bible-believing world, these doctrines stand as an evidence that Joseph Smith was a prophet and that ours is an ancient church restored. . . . These doctrines, of such importance to the ancient Saints, have been restored once again to a place of prominence among the Saints of the latter days."[15]

Biblical References to Man's Premortal Existence

Nephi saw in vision the day when the "great and abominable church" would be involved in eliminating from the holy scriptures those simple truths and teachings that they neither believed nor desired that others embrace. Nephi said:

They have taken away from the gospel of the Lamb many parts which are plain and most precious; and also many covenants of the Lord have they taken away.

And all this have they done that they might pervert the right ways of the Lord, that they might blind the eyes and harden the hearts of the children of men.

. . . Because of the many plain and precious things which have been taken out of the book, which were plain unto the understanding of the children of men, according to the plainness which is in the Lamb of God—because of these things which are taken away out of the gospel of the Lamb, an exceedingly great many do stumble, yea, insomuch that Satan hath great power over them. (1 Nephi 13:26–27, 29.)

Surely the doctrine of man's premortal relationship to God was among the "plain and precious" doctrines that were lost from the scriptures during the dark period of apostasy that prevailed during the first few centuries after Christ. The disappearance from canon of the doctrine of premortal life was virtually completed by A.D. 543 when the pope's council, convened by Justinian, labeled such teaching as heresy. Despite the adversary's efforts, as seen by Nephi, to remove such "plain and precious" teachings from the Bible, there remain glimpses of man's premortal role in both the Old and New Testaments. While not understood by much of the world and misinterpreted by most of Christianity, these scanty scriptural glimpses, when coupled with modern revelation, provide valuable insight into man's spiritual origin.

Jeremiah was told by the Lord, "Before I formed thee in the belly I knew thee; and before thou camest forth out of the womb I sanctified thee, and I ordained thee a prophet unto the nations" (Jeremiah 1:5). This Old Testament passage has troubled biblical scholars for generations. Some have said that it is merely evidence of God's omniscience or foreknowledge. Others have suggested that it is only symbolic or poetic language. A few Christian scholars admit that there may be something to the idea that Jeremiah existed in some way prior to his birth which would allow God to know him beforehand. "The idea of preexistence means only that in some manner a person existed before his or her incarnation on earth," wrote one Christian scholar in referring to God's foreknowledge of Jeremiah. "This question was hotly debated by Christians of late antiquity, and the faction of the Church which was bitterly opposed to preexistence gained the upper hand. By the sixth century belief in preexistence was declared heresy. All of this is quite astonishing in view of the clear and repeated biblical evidence for preexistence."[16]

Even one of the earliest Christian theologians, Clement of Alexandria, recognized the significance of this passage in Jeremiah as it relates to man's foreordination. He suggested, "It is possible that in speaking these things the prophet [Jeremiah] is referring to us, as being known to God as faithful before the foundation of the world. Only now have we become babes for the purposes of fulfilling the plan of God."[17] Another theologian also asserts that Jeremiah's "prenatal" calling applies not only to God's chosen prophets but also to all Christians. "It is revealed to him [Jeremiah] that God's selection and purpose go back to his prenatal life and conception. The choice was from the beginning, the plan was predetermined. Before his birth, he was chosen, set aside, and appointed to the prophetic office. As with the prophet, so with the Christian. There is a divine plan which is prior, not only to our response, but also to our existence."[18]

Theologians continue their debate and their efforts to refute the notion that Jeremiah did, indeed, live in some premortal state. However, a look at the Lord's use of three specific words—*knew, sanctified, ordained*—indicates that this scriptural passage can be taken literally. These terms are related, and, in fact, are significant steps in a spiritual process. The Lord *knew* Jeremiah prior to his birth and was familiar with his spiritual attitudes and abilities. Because of that knowledge and because of Jeremiah's premortal faith, obedience, and valiance in defending and sustaining the predetermined plan, he was *sanctified*. With this prenatal sanctification he was then prepared to actually be *ordained* a prophet to ancient Judah even before his birth. These are steps in the process of foreordination, of which we learn from modern revelation. Foreordination will be discussed in chapter 7; but the Lord's words to Jeremiah, as seen in the Old Testament, offer a glimpse of man's premortal life.

There are numerous other biblical references whose true meaning would be lost to the world without the assistance of modern revelation and the teachings of living prophets. One such reference is the Lord's question to Job: "Where wast thou when I laid the foundations of the earth?" The answer came when God spoke of a glorious premortal day when "all the sons of God shouted for joy" (Job 38:4, 7). Why would God ask Job where he was during this event, if Job had not also had a prior existence? If *all* the sons of God shouted for joy, did not God consider Jeremiah—the worthy, sanctified and chosen prophet of God—also a son of God who also shouted for joy?

Ecclesiastes speaks of the immortal nature of man as evidenced in death. "Then shall the dust *return* to the earth as it was: and the spirit shall *return* unto God who gave it" (Ecclesiastes 12:7; italics added). How can a spirit return to a place or a state of being where it has not been before?

Moses made several references that imply a premortal life. In praying, he spoke of God as "the God of the spirits of all flesh" (Numbers 16:22; 27:16). On another occasion, he spoke of a premortal day "when the most High divided to the nations their inheritance, when he separated the sons of Adam, he set the bounds of the people according to the number of the children of Israel" (Deuteronomy 32:8). Elder James E. Talmage commented on this passage: "From this we learn that the earth was allotted to the nations, according to the number of the children of Israel; it is evident therefore that the number was known prior to the existence of the Israelitish nation in the flesh; this is most easily explained on the basis of a previous existence in which the spirits of the future nation were known."[19]

Just as Job learned that before the earth was formed all the sons of God shouted for joy, there are also several references to men on earth as being those sons—spiritual children of God. A Psalm of Asaph says, "Ye are gods; and all of you are children of the Most High" (Psalm 82:6). Moses spoke of the children of Israel as "children of the Lord your God" (Deuteronomy 14:1). Hosea the prophet spoke of ancient Israel as "sons of the living God" (Hosea 1:10). No doubt these "sons of God" and "children of God" were with Job and Jeremiah and all the offspring of God who shouted for joy in a premortal abode. The question posed by the Lord to Job, "Where wast thou when I laid the foundations of the earth?" begins to be answered with these scriptural glimpses from the Old Testament.

One of the recurring themes of the New Testament is the premortal role of Jesus Christ as the "Lamb slain from [before] the foundation of the world" (Revelation 13:8). Numerous references give evidence of Christ's own premortal life. Referring to Christ as the Word, John records that "in the beginning was the Word, and the Word was with God, and the Word was God. . . . And all things were made by him" (John 1:1, 3; see also Revelation 19:13–16; D&C 93:6–9). On at least two occasions, the Savior himself referred to his premortal existence. In speaking to the Jews regarding Father Abraham, Jesus told them that Abraham had seen and rejoiced in Jesus' day and mission. Not understanding, they queried Jesus as to how he could have seen Abraham, who had died long ago. He responded, "Verily, verily I say unto you, Before Abraham was, I am" (John 8:56–58). His use of the term "I Am" is the same as that used in identifying Jehovah in Exodus 3:14. Undoubtedly, Jesus was referring to his premortal role as Jehovah. Therefore his response to the Jews could better be translated as, "Before Abraham, was I, I am [Jehovah]."

In his great intercessory prayer, Jesus once again speaks of his premortal existence when he prays unto the Father to "glorify thou me with thine own self with the glory which I had with thee before the world was" (John 17:5). Today, virtually all Christians acknowledge the premortal life and immortal godship of Jesus Christ. Certainly Peter recognized Christ's premortality when he wrote that Christ was "foreordained before the foundation of the world" (1 Peter 1:19–20). The confusion, however, arises regarding a possible parallel between Christ's premortal life and mankind's. Commenting on the New Testament evidence for premortal existence, another Christian scholar has written:

> Implicit in all these [scriptural] statements is the recognition that the majesty and greatness of Christ are of such an order as to precede and outlast secular time. It is perfectly apparent that Christ exists eternally and indestructibly. Nor does his existence in any way depend upon the presence of the body.
>
> The preexistence of Christ does not, of course, guarantee the preexistence of the human soul. However, to the extent that Christ presents himself as an attainable example to mankind, human preexistence is not to be dismissed. If Christ is an example for man in his works, then why not in his stature as well?[20]

While the premortal life of Christ does not prove the premortal life of all men, there is much scriptural evidence to indicate that others too have existed from before the foundation of the world. Paul, on several occasions, preached that Christ was the "firstborn of every creature" (Colossians 1:15), the Father's "firstbegotten into the world" (Hebrews 1:6), and the "firstborn among many brethren" (Romans 8:29). Since Christ was not the firstborn of God's physical or mortal creations, how can Paul be referring to anything other than Christ's preeminent role as firstborn of all of God's spirit children? Elder Orson Pratt summarized the significance of these passages as they refer to man's as well as Christ's premortal existence.

> Have you not read, in the New Testament, that Jesus Christ was the first-born of every creature? From this reading it would seem that he was the oldest of the whole human family, that is, so far as his birth in the spirit world is concerned. . . . Have you not also read in the New Testament that he is called our elder brother? Does this refer to

the birth of the body of flesh and bones? By no means, for there were hundreds of millions who were born upon our earth before the body of flesh and bones was born whom we call Jesus. How is it, then, that he is our elder brother? We must go back to the previous birth, before the foundation of this earth; we have to go back to past ages, to the period when he was begotten of the Father among the great family of spirits.[21]

Another episode in the life of Christ gives an interesting glimpse of the doctrine of premortal life in the New Testament. Upon approaching a man who had been born blind, the disciples asked Jesus, "Master, who did sin, this man, or his parents, that he was born blind?" (John 9:2.) The question itself, along with Jesus' answer, implies a premortal life for the blind man. It is interesting to note the commentaries of those both in and out of the Church regarding this episode. One non-LDS scholar acknowledges that the disciples' question demonstrates their belief in a premortal existence of mankind.

> In interpreting this episode, commentators have pointed out that the example of the man blind from birth is occasionally used to illustrate the problem of divine justice. How can we grasp the justice of an all-loving God, if he will allow a man to enter into the world with such a crushing handicap? . . .
>
> The answer that Jesus gives to the question of the disciples shows that he is much more interested in "making manifest the works of God" than he is in the origins or cause of the man's blindness. Nevertheless, there is a glaring inconsistency in the question posed by the disciples. They ask the Lord if the man himself could have committed the sin that led to his blindness. Given the fact that the man has been blind from birth, we are confronted with a provocative question. When could he have made such transgressions as to make him blind at birth? *The only conceivable answer is in some prenatal state. The question posed by the disciples explicitly presupposed prenatal existence.* It will be also

noted that Christ says nothing to dispel or correct the presupposition. *Here is incontrovertible support for a doctrine of human preexistence.*

It is perfectly reasonable to surmise on the basis of this episode that Jesus and his followers accepted preexistence and thought so little of it that the question of prenatal sin did not even call for an answer.[22]

Elder Bruce R. McConkie has also commented on their obvious acceptance of the doctrine:

> Apparently the Jews had some understanding of the doctrine of pre-existence. Among their righteous forebears it had been taught plainly as a basic gospel truth. . . . Such scriptures as were then available to them, however, contained only passing allusions to it. . . . But it was a doctrine implicit in the whole plan of salvation as such was known to and understood by them. They had, for instance, no more occasion to prove the ante-mortal existence of spirits than they did to prove God was a personal Being. Both truths were assumed; concepts to the contrary were heresies which gained prevalence in later ages.
>
> Jesus' disciples—probably as a direct result of his teachings—knew and believed that men were the spirit children of God in preexistence and that in such prior estate they were subject to law and endowed with agency. Otherwise they never would have asked nor would there have been any sense or reason to a question which is predicated upon the assumption that men can sin before they are born into mortality.[23]

There are many other teachings and examples in the New Testament which afford glimpses of man's spiritual origins and which are implications of his premortal life. Most of the Christian world either ignores or grossly misinterprets these biblical passages. Examples include Paul's teachings on God's foreknowledge and foreordination of men and nations (see Acts 17:26; Romans 9:4–11; Ephesians 4:1), his controversial use of the term "predestinate" (Romans 8:29), and his explanation of the "election" of Israel and the doctrine of adoption (Romans 11). Paul's statements that man is the "off-spring of God" (Acts 17:29; Romans 8:16) and that God is the "Father of spirits" (Hebrews 12:9; Ephesians 4:6) are also important indications of man's spiritual lineage which cannot be fully comprehended without a belief in the premortal existence. In addition to Paul, Jude and John have also described the War in Heaven where angels "kept not their first estate" (Jude 1:6) and where Michael and his angels fought against Lucifer (Revelation 12:7; see also Isaiah 14:13; Luke 10:18).

While these many references may only be shadowy remnants of a doctrine lost from Christianity, they help to bring the doctrine of man's premortal existence out of scriptural obscurity when coupled with modern scriptures and the teachings of latter-day prophets.

Plain and Precious Truths Restored

Just as Nephi foresaw the loss of many of the plain and precious teachings in the Bible, he also envisioned the latter-day restoration of those truths. He saw "other books, which came forth by the power of the Lamb . . . unto the convincing of the Gentiles and the remnant of the seed of my brethren, and also the Jews who were scattered upon all the face of the earth, that the records of the prophets and of the twelve apostles of the Lamb are true" (1 Nephi 13:39). An angel informed Nephi that these "last records" would not only establish the truth of the ancient scriptures, but would also "make known the plain and precious things which have been taken away from them" (1 Nephi 13:40).

When the heavens were opened to the Prophet Joseph Smith, the floodgates of knowledge concerning man's premortal relationship to a Heavenly Father were likewise opened. Previously there were only glimpses, but the restoration of the gospel opened the windows of heaven to a vivid view of man's premortal life. The Book of Mormon, latter-day revelations contained in the Doctrine and Covenants, and the visions of Moses and Abraham in the Pearl of Great Price contributed much indeed to the restoration of this "plain and precious" doctrine.

The Nephite prophet Alma taught that those holding the priesthood had been "called and prepared from the foundation of the world according to the foreknowledge of God." He further taught that this foreordination in the "first place" came as a result of their "exceeding faith and good works" (Alma 13:3). This concept of foreordination will be examined in greater detail in chapter 7, but this passage demonstrates how the Book of Mormon illuminates this important doctrine which was only suggested in the teachings of Jeremiah and the Apostle Paul.

Moses saw in vision that God "created all things . . . spiritually, before they were naturally upon the face of the earth" (Moses 3:5). Later Moses also described Satan's premortal rebellion and expulsion from heaven. This latter-day revelation provided the lost details of this premortal event which had only been alluded to in the prophecies of Isaiah and John the Revelator (see Moses 4:1–4).

Enoch saw the "spirits that God had created" (Moses 6:36). Abraham beheld a glorious vision of the spirits or "intelligences that were organized before the world was; and among all these there were many of the noble and great ones" (Abraham 3:22). Abraham also discovered, as did Jeremiah, that he was known and chosen by God even before he came to earth. "And God saw these souls that they were good," records Abraham, "and he stood in the midst of them, and he said: These I will make my rulers; *for he stood among those that were spirits*, and he saw that they were good; and he said unto me: Abraham, thou art one of them; thou wast chosen before thou wast born" (Abraham 3:23; italics added).

Joseph Smith also received many revelations that included insight and information pertaining to man's premortality. We learn that "the devil was before Adam" and that as a result of his premortal rebellion "a third part of the hosts of heaven turned he away" from God, and "they were thrust down and thus became the devil and his angels" (D&C 29:36–37).

Joseph learned from the Savior himself that man was created "before the world was made" (D&C 49:17) and was among "all the seraphic hosts of heaven, before the world was made" (D&C 38:1). He later learned that just as Christ, the Word, was with God in the beginning, "man was also in the beginning with God. . . . For man is spirit. The elements are eternal, and spirit and element, inseparably connected." (D&C 93:29, 33.)

President Joseph F. Smith provided additional prophetic insight in his vision of the redemption of the dead (D&C 138). While seeing the departed spirits of faithful men and women, he also learned that these same spirits were "among the noble and great ones who were chosen in the beginning to be rulers in the Church of God." He further learned that these spirits had "received their first lessons in the world of spirits and were prepared to come forth in the due time of the Lord to labor in his vineyard for the salvation of the souls of men" (D&C 138:55–56).

While theologians and philosophers continue to speculate about man's premortal existence, latter-day prophets and apostles have emphatically confirmed the doctrine with their inspired utterances. Virtually every prophet in this dispensation has spoken plainly of man's premortal life and has provided valuable glimpses of that premortal realm.

The Prophet Joseph Smith spoke of the eternal nature of the spirit of man. He taught that "the spirit of man is not a created being; it existed from eternity, and will exist to eternity. Anything created cannot be eternal. . . . The Father called all spirits before Him at the creation of man, and organized them."[24]

President Wilford Woodruff later confirmed that all mankind dwelt with God prior to this life. "With regard to our position before we came here," recorded President Woodruff, "I will say that we dwelt with the Father and with the Son. . . . We dwelt in the presence of God before we came here."[25] President Brigham Young also agreed not only that our spirits lived prior to our physical birth but also that we were all intimately familiar with God. "I want to tell you, each and every one of you, that you are well acquainted with God our heavenly Father, or the great Eloheim. You are all well acquainted with Him, for there is not a soul of you but what has lived in His house and dwelt with Him year after year; and yet you are seeking to become acquainted with Him, when the fact is, you have merely forgotten what you did know."[26] President Joseph F. Smith has reminded us that we were with Job and the other children of God prior to our birth when "all the sons of God shouted for joy" and that we had good reason to rejoice. "Where did we come from? From God. Our spirits existed before they came to this world. They were in the councils of the heavens before the foundations of the earth were laid. *We* were there. We sang together with the heavenly hosts for joy, when the foundations of the earth were laid, and when the plan of our existence upon this earth and redemption were mapped out. We were there; we were interested, and we took a part in this great preparation."[27]

The theological mystery of man's spiritual origins was resolved by the First Presidency of the Church in this official statement of doctrine:

Inquiries arise from time to time respecting the attitude of the Church of Jesus Christ of Latter-day Saints upon questions which . . . are closely connected with the fundamental principles of salvation. The latest inquiry of this kind that has reached us is in relation to the origin of man. It is believed that a statement of the position held by the Church upon this important subject will be timely and productive of good. . . .

The Church of Jesus Christ of Latter-day Saints, basing its belief on divine revelation, ancient and modern, proclaims man to be the direct and lineal offspring of Deity. . . . By His almighty power He organized the earth, and all that it contains, from spirit and element, which exist co-eternally with Himself. . . .

Man is the child of God, formed in the divine image and endowed with divine attributes.[28]

The doctrine of man's premortal relationship to and existence with Deity might well be compared to a giant jigsaw puzzle. There are hundreds, if not thousands, of pieces in the picture. References to the doctrine in literature, philosophy, and theology provide only a very few glimpses of the entire scene. Teachings of the early Christian leaders and apocryphal writings supply a few more pieces of the puzzle. The biblical references and allusions to this important truth fill in yet a few more of the gaps. But, still, there are only isolated and scattered glimpses. So scanty are the references that many do not see any details of the picture; or they misinterpret what they see, as if they are viewing a giant puzzle with only a handful of pieces fitted together. It is not until the "plain and precious" pieces are added that the picture becomes clearer. Elder Boyd K. Packer has explained that "there is no way to make sense out of life without a knowledge of the doctrine of premortal life. The idea that mortal birth is the beginning is preposterous. There is no way to explain life if you believe that. The notion that life ends with mortal death is ridiculous. There is no way to face life if you believe that. When we understand the doctrine of premortal life, then things fit together and make sense."[29]

With the restoration of the gospel, many additional pieces of the puzzle have been fitted together. The picture that was only partially distinguishable has now become clear. To Latter-day Saints, there is no question that we did, indeed, live before this life. There are, however, many questions in the minds of Latter-day Saints concerning the nature of that existence.

What is intelligence?

Is man literally a child of God? How can that be?

What was the premortal existence like? What did we do there?

What laws and conditions prevailed there?

Was there really a premortal war in heaven?

Were there differences among the spirits?

What accounted for those differences?

What is foreordination? How does it operate?

Why can't I remember anything about that premortal world?

How does my experience there affect my life here?

Why is it so important to understand the nature of the premortal existence?

These and many other aspects of our premortal life are part of the overall picture of man's premortal life. While not all of the pieces of the puzzle have been revealed, there is much in scripture, in modern revelation, and in the teachings of the living prophets that provides us with additional glimpses of the premortal existence.

Notes

1. Papias, in *Patrologiae Cursus Completus . . . Series Graeca*, 5:1260, as cited in Hugh Nibley, *The World and the Prophets* (Salt Lake City: Deseret Book Co., 1974), p. 226.

2. Clement, in *Patrologiae . . . Graeca*, 8:321, as cited in Hugh Nibley, *The World and the Prophets*, p. 228.

3. St. Augustine, "On the Immortality of the Soul," in *The World's Great Thinkers, Man and Spirit: The Speculative Philosophers*, edited by Saxe Commins and Robert N. Linscott (New York: Random House, 1947), pp. 3–4.

4. Tertullian, *Apologeticus* . . . , in *Patrologiae* . . . *Graeca*, 1:307–308, as cited in Hugh Nibley, *The World and the Prophets*, p. 229; italics added.

5. Hugh Nibley, *The World and the Prophets*, p. 229.

6. Origen, *Peri Archon*, in *Patrologiae* . . . *Graeca*, 9:230–231, as cited in Hugh Nibley, *The World and the Prophets*, p. 230.

7. Geoffrey Hodson, *Reincarnation, Fact or Fallacy? An Examination and Exposition of the Doctrine of Rebirth* (Wheaton, Illinois: The Theosophical Publishing House, 1967), pp. 14–15. For additional information on Origen's teachings and the Council of 543 A.D., see Quincy Howe, Jr., *Reincarnation for the Christian* (Philadelphia: Westminster Press, 1974), pp. 62–84.

8. Jacob Boehme, *The Doctrine of Jacob Boehme*, compiled by Franz Hartman (New York: 1928), p. 52, as quoted by Gary W. Ellsworth, "Trailing Clouds of Glory—Poets and Philosophers Examine the Preexistence," *Ensign*, October 1974, p. 51.

9. Flavius Josephus, *Antiquities of the Jews*, 15:371; *Jewish Wars*, 2:154–156.

10. R. H. Charles, *The Apocrypha and Pseudepigrapha of the Old Testament*, 2 vols. (Oxford: Oxford University, Clarendon Press, 1976), 2:444.

11. Hugh Nibley, *Old Testament and Related Studies* (Salt Lake City: Deseret Book Co. and The Foundation for Ancient Research and Mormon Studies), pp. 156–157; see also pp. 174–175.

12. Hugh Nibley, *Old Testament and Related Studies*, p. 157.

13. Hugh Nibley, *Old Testament and Related Studies*, p. 158.

14. Joseph Fielding McConkie, "Pre-Mortal Existence, Foreordinations and Heavenly Councils," ch. 9 in *Apocryphal Writings and the Latter-day Saints* (Provo, Utah: Religious Studies Center, Brigham Young University, 1986), pp. 183–184.

15. Joseph Fielding McConkie, in *Apocryphal Writings and the Latter-day Saints*, pp. 194–195.

16. William de Arteaga, *Past Life Visions: A Christian Exploration* (New York: Seabury Press, 1983), p. 127.

17. Clement of Alexandria, *Paedogogus*, in *Patrologiae* . . . *Graeca*, 8:321, as quoted by Hugh Nibley, *The World and the Prophets*, p. 228; italics added.

18. Stephen Winward, *A Guide to the Prophets* (Atlanta: John Knox Press, 1976), p. 123; italics added.

19. James E. Talmage, *The Articles of Faith* (Salt Lake City: The Church of Jesus Christ of Latter-day Saints, 1977), p. 193.

20. Howe, *Reincarnation for the Christian*, pp. 96–97.

21. Orson Pratt, in *Journal of Discourses*, 18:290.

22. Howe, *Reincarnation for the Christian*, pp. 92–93.

23. Bruce R. McConkie, *Doctrinal New Testament Commentary*, 3 vols. (Salt Lake City: Bookcraft, 1965–73), 1:480.

24. Joseph Smith, *History of the Church*, (Salt Lake City: Deseret Book Co., 1967), 3:387.

25. Wilford Woodruff, *Millennial Star*, 56:229, as quoted in *Doctrines from the Prophets*, compiled by Alma P. Burton (Salt Lake City: Bookcraft, 1970), p. 265.

26. Brigham Young, in *Journal of Discourses*, 4:216.

27. Joseph F. Smith, in *Journal of Discourses*, 25:57.

28. First Presidency statement, Joseph F. Smith, John R. Winder, Anthon H. Lund, in *Improvement Era*, November 1909, pp. 75–81.

29. Boyd K. Packer, in Conference Report, October 1983, p. 22.

3

Intelligence or Intelligences?

In 1833 the Lord revealed to the Prophet Joseph Smith that "man was also in the beginning with God. Intelligence, or the light of truth, was not created or made, neither indeed can be." (D&C 93:29.) Several years later, with the publication of the book of Abraham, additional information about the immortality of the soul of man came to light. Abraham says that he was shown by the Lord "the intelligences that were organized before the world was" (Abraham 3:22). The Lord also told Abraham that these intelligences or spirits "have no beginning; they existed before, they shall have no end, they shall exist after, for they are gnolaum, or eternal" (Abraham 3:18).

The Prophet Joseph often refuted the *ex nihilo* ("creation out of nothing") doctrine that was popular among the sects of his day. The Prophet suggested that just as the earth could not be created out of nothing, neither could man. In 1839, he taught, "The Spirit of Man is not a created being; it existed from Eternity and will exist to eternity. Anything created cannot be Eternal. And earth, water, etc.—all these had their existence in an elementary State from Eternity."[1]

The Prophet had previously learned by way of revelation that "the elements are eternal" (D&C 93:33). No doubt he understood this to apply to both the physical creation of the earth and the physical bodies of men, but what about the immortal "Spirit of Man" of which Joseph spoke? What was meant by the phrase "in an elementary state"?

In April of 1844, the Prophet Joseph once again addressed the subject of the immortality of the spirit of man and its relationship to God. This address has come to be known as the King Follett Discourse.

> The soul—the mind of man—the immortal spirit. Where did it come from? All learned men and doctors of divinity say that God created it in the beginning; but it is not so: the very idea lessens man in my estimation. . . .
>
> We say that God himself is a self-existent being. Who told you so? It is correct enough; but how did it get into your heads? Who told you that man did not exist in like manner upon the same principles? Man does exist upon the same principles. . . .
>
> The mind or the intelligence which man possesses is co-equal [co-eternal] with God himself. . . .
>
> I am dwelling on the immortality of the spirit of man. Is it logical to say that the intelligence of spirits is immortal, and yet that it had a beginning? The intelligence of spirits had no beginning, neither will it have an end. . . .
>
> Intelligence is eternal and exists upon a self-existent principle. It is a spirit from age to age, and there is no creation about it.[2]

It is interesting to note the various terms used by the Prophet in this discourse in referring to the immortal spirit of man. Earlier, he had taught that man had existed eternally in "an elementary state." The King Follett Discourse seems to define more precisely what that "elementary state" means. Present in Nauvoo when Joseph delivered this sermon were four eminent recorders—Willard Richards, Wilford Woodruff, William Clayton, and Thomas Bullock. A careful examination of the recorded notes of each of these men reveals the many terms used by the Prophet to refer to man's immortality. These terms include "soul," "mind of man," "spirit," "intelligent part," and "first principles of man." Only Wilford Woodruff recorded that Joseph used the plural term "intelligences."[3]

This portion of the discourse has generated considerable discussion and debate from 1844 to the present. Many interpretations have arisen. Even today it is not precisely clear what Joseph meant by "intelligence," "mind of man," or "elementary state." There is, at least, no question that the Prophet Joseph taught that there is an element of man that was not created but has existed eternally—the same eternal element identified in Doctrine and Covenants 93:29.

From the days of Nauvoo to this day, questions remain concerning the nature of that eternal existence of man. What is "intelligence"? Did we exist as "intelligences" prior to our spirit birth? Did individual entities possess unique characteristics, personalities, and intellectual and spiritual capacities *prior* to being spirits? Was there individual agency in a "prespirit" existence?

These questions have been discussed and debated at great length by some of the greatest theologians, scholars, and critical thinkers in the history of the Church. While there is agreement on most of the important doctrinal points pertaining to man's eternal nature and premortal life, differing views continue on the nature of "intelligence" versus "intelligences." Today there are two basic schools of thought on the question of the eternal mind of man as generated by the Prophet's Nauvoo discourse.

School of Thought No. 1: Intelligence, the Primal Element

Man did not exist as a separate, individual intelligence prior to spirit birth; the spirit was "organized" from uncreated eternal elements known as "intelligence."

Early leaders of the Church, including Brigham Young, felt that man was "organized" by God from an eternal, uncreated "spirit element." The teaching prevailed that man, as an individual, premortal entity, did *not* exist prior to a literal spiritual birth.[4]

This interpretation is seen in the writings and sermons of some of the early leaders of the Church. One such leader who reflected this view was Parley P. Pratt. He wrote that man as an individual entity or "organized intelligence" was brought forth from an uncreated, eternal, primal spiritual matter. "They are organized intelligences. What are they made of? They are made of the element which we call spirit. . . . Let a given quantity of this element, thus endowed, or capacitated, be organized in the size and form of man . . . what would we call this individual, organized portion of the spiritual element? We would call it a spiritual body, an individual intelligence, an agent endowed with life, with a degree of independence, or inherent will, with the powers of motion, of thought, and with the attributes of moral, intellectual, and sympathetic affections and emotions."[5]

In 1884, Elder Charles W. Penrose, commenting on the eternal nature of God, made an interesting observation that also has important bearing on the eternal nature of man. He said:

> If God is an individual spirit and dwells in a body, the question will arise, "Is He the Eternal Father?" Yes, He is the Eternal Father. "Is it a fact that He never had a beginning?" In the *elementary particles* of his organism, He did not. But if He is an organized Being, there must have been a time when that being was organized. This, some one will say, would infer that God had a beginning. This spirit which pervades all things, which is the light and life of all things, by which our heavenly Father operates, by which He is omnipotent, never had a beginning and never will have an end. It is the light of truth; it is the *spirit of intelligence*.

Applying this same concept to the eternal nature of man, Elder Penrose went on to say that "the individual, the organized person may have had a beginning, but that spirit of which and by which they [were] organized never had a beginning. . . . The *primal particles* never had a beginning. They have been organized in different shapes [as individual entities]; the organism [individual spirit] had a beginning, but the elements or atoms of which it is composed never had. . . . The *elementary parts of matter as well as of spirit*, using ordinary terms, never had a beginning."[6]

Taking Elder Penrose's comments further, it may be appropriate to use a scientific analogy to summarize his views. Man's physical body is comprised of numerous elements or "elementary parts of matter." The scriptures teach that these "elements are eternal" (D&C 93:33). Even though the elements of carbon, hydrogen, oxygen, and many others that have been "organized" to form the body of man have always existed, it would be unreasonable to assume that they have eternally existed only as elements unique to that person.

What is this spirit element that is often referred to as "intelligence" or the "mind of man"? It is interesting to note Elder Penrose's description of intelligence as the primal element of man. He used phrases such as "pervades all things" and "light of all things." This corresponds with the Lord's own description of the "light of Christ" as seen in Doctrine and Covenants 88:7–13. "The light which shineth, which giveth you light, is through him who enlighteneth your eyes, which is the same light that quickeneth your understandings; . . . The light which is in all things, which giveth life to all things, which is the law by which all things are governed, even the power of God."

This eternal power, the Light of Christ, may be the power that works upon that primal spirit element from which man's spirit was created. The Light of Christ as a power that enlightens and quickens the mind may also be the "mind of man" of which the Prophet Joseph spoke as being eternal and uncreated. Parley P. Pratt also spoke of "inherent properties" of the Light of Christ that may relate to the primal part of the mind and spirit of man. Referring to the Light of Christ, he said: "Its inherent properties embrace all the attributes of intelligence and affection. It is endowed with wisdom, knowledge, truth, love, charity, justice, and mercy, in all their ramifications. In short, it is the attributes of the eternal power and Godhead?"[7] "We know, however, that there is something called intelligence which always existed," wrote President Joseph Fielding Smith more recently. "It is the real eternal part of man, which was not created or made. This intelligence *combined with the spirit* constitutes a spiritual identity or individual."[8]

In 1967, Elder Bruce R. McConkie taught a summer seminar for religious educators at Brigham Young University. In his lecture, Elder McConkie addressed the topic of intelligence and its relationship to the eternal nature of mankind.

> ... If I evaluate this correctly, this spirit matter or spirit element—the revelation used the word "matter"—it would be in effect the equivalent of elements as we use the terms, and we are trying to get words to get the concept over. This spirit element was born as a spirit being or offspring. Or in other words, this thing that is called intelligence was organized into *intelligences* who were *spirits*.... Now what I am saying is that intelligence and spirit matter seem to be equated as the same thing, and that intelligences and spirits seem to be the same thing, and the organization of intelligence into intelligences, and the birth of spirit matter, which is the same thing, is a birth into a state of spirits.[9]

While not officially speaking for the Church, Elder McConkie later gave additional information concerning this matter. In response to a letter from Walter Horne, Elder McConkie answered the following question: "Is it official Church doctrine, affirmed by the living prophet and all of the presiding Brethren, that we had no identity, that we were not individual intelligent entities before we were born into the spirit world?"

> As to official Church pronouncements on doctrinal points, they are almost nonexistent. . . .

As far as I know there is no official pronouncement on the subject at hand. . . .

In my judgment, spirit element exists and it was organized into spirit beings, or in other words intelligence exists and it became the intelligences that were organized. In my judgment there was no agency prior to spirit birth and we did not exist as (individual) entities until that time. I do know that this matter has arisen perhaps six or eight times that I have been here and have been involved in reading and approving priesthood and auxiliary lessons. In each of these instances, the matter was deleted from the lesson. In each case it was expressly stated that we have no knowledge of any existence earlier than our existence as the spirit children of God.[10]

As Elder McConkie carefully pointed out in this letter, the Church has not officially resolved this issue. It has never officially or specifically clarified what the Prophet Joseph Smith meant in the King Follett Discourse when he referred to the immortal "intelligence of spirits" and the "co-equal [co-eternal] mind of man." Lacking this official doctrinal clarification, many continue to hold differing views on the subject. Despite the fact that Elder McConkie's views represent the traditional views of the Church and its early leaders, there has been and continues to be a second view or school of thought regarding the eternal nature of the spirit of man.

School of Thought No. 2: Intelligences, the Pre-Spirit Entities of Man

Each person has existed eternally. Prior to spirit birth people existed as individual intelligences with unique characteristics and capacities, inherently able to be enlarged upon through agency.

Elder Orson Pratt often argued eloquently, though controversially, that neither God nor man was created, but that both God and man have always existed. Basing his views on the earlier statements of the Prophet Joseph, Elder Pratt felt that man, as an individual entity or intelligence, had always existed, but in a different—more basic or primal—state. He differed with Brigham Young with respect to the nature of that primal state. While President Young, Elder Penrose, and others argued that this state of "intelligence" was a collective elementary state, Orson Pratt felt strongly that it was indeed a highly individualized existence. He proposed that "each particle [or intelligence] eternally existed prior to this organization; each was enabled to perceive its own existence; each had the power of self-motion; each was an intelligent, living being of itself. . . . In this independent, separate condition, it was capable of being governed by laws adapted to the amount of knowledge and experience it had gained during its past eternal experience."[11]

In 1865 the First Presidency issued a statement which stated that Elder Pratt's views of the eternal nature of God and man were not to be construed as the official doctrine of the Church. They made the statement that members of the Church, along with all the "Prophets and Apostles," would have to be "content with the knowledge that from all eternity there had existed organized beings, in an organized form."[12]

This seemed to settle the issue—at least temporarily. The accepted doctrinal view was that man, as an individual entity, came about from the organization of the primal element, intelligence, at the time of his spirit birth. This view prevailed, virtually unchallenged until the early twentieth century. Elder B. H. Roberts, President of the First Quorum of the Seventy, articulated a view somewhat similar to the views of Orson Pratt. This idea has sometimes been labeled as "Personal Eternalism." Elder Roberts claimed that man existed as a personal, individual, self-conscious entity prior to spirit birth. He identified these entities as "intelligences." These intelligences were different from the intelligences that Abraham saw in vision, however, in that the scriptural intelligences were organized spirits (see Abraham 3:22). Elder Roberts wrote:

> There is a complex thing we call man, an intelligent entity, uncreated, self-existent, indestructible, he—for that entity is a person; because as we shall see he is possessed with powers that go with the person. . . .
>
> Under this concept, the eternal ego of man was, in some past age of the other world dim to us, clothed with a spiritual body. That was man's spiritual birth and his entrance into the spiritual world. . . . The term "an intelligence" is then applied to the eternal ego of man existing even before the spiritual creation. . . .
>
> The difference then between "spirits" and "intelligences," as here used, is this: Spirits are uncreated intelligences inhabiting spiritual bodies; while "intelligences," pure and simple, are intelligent entities, but unembodied in either spirit bodies or bodies of flesh and bone. They are uncreated, self-existent entities. . . .[13]

The views of Elder Roberts, a gifted and prolific writer, were published in several different sources and disseminated widely throughout the Church. While Elder Roberts never claimed that his views were anything but his own ideas, they nonetheless took on a "quasi-official" status. Perhaps this status can be attributed primarily to his article "Immortality of Man" which was published in the April 1907 *Improvement Era.* An editorial comment prefaced this article which may have made it somewhat difficult for some readers to determine whether or not Elder Roberts's views officially represented the Church. The editors commented, "Elder Roberts submitted the following paper to the First Presidency and a number of the Twelve Apostles, none of whom found anything objectionable in it, or contrary to the revealed word of God, and therefore favor its publication."[14]

Although the Brethren favored the publication of this article, it was not to be construed as an endorsement of Elder Roberts's views. In fact, Elder Roberts himself specifically stated that the ideas he presented were not official doctrine.

Undoubtedly, if the Lord has anything further just now to reveal to the Church upon that or any other subject, it will, of course, be revealed through the . . . President of the Church. My purpose in mentioning the foregoing remark at this point is that I may correct any idea that may be entertained by anyone, and in howsoever slight degree, that what I have written, or what I shall now write, on this or any other subject, is given out as the doctrine of the Church. I am in no way deluded with the idea that my writings are setting forth in any authoritative way the doctrines of the Church.[15]

While Elder Roberts's views may not have been "contrary to the revealed word of God," they were not necessarily in harmony with the revelations, either. As he stated, he was merely presenting his own personal view or interpretation of the revelations concerning the immortality of man. Despite Elder Roberts's own specific cautions, however, many members of the Church felt that because this idea had been published in a Church magazine it was the official doctrine of the Church. In the succeeding years many of these views found place in Church curriculum and in books by prominent LDS philosophers and educators. Many forgot that Elder Roberts himself had said, "What I have written . . . are my views." As Elder Bruce R. McConkie said, "As far as I know there is no official pronouncement on the subject at hand, but that applies also to a thousand other subjects. . . . We are not going to say categorically that this is true or this is false. But I will suggest that some of the things that are said in the Church are in the realm of speculation and can't be definitely and categorically known so far as the revelations are concerned."[16]

Referring specifically to the school of thought promoted by the views of Elder B. H. Roberts, Elder McConkie gave this cautious assessment: "I don't say it is false, I just say it is in the realm of speculation."[17]

Conclusion

There are many things connected with man's premortal origin that the Lord has not yet seen fit to reveal. However, he has revealed, in modern scriptures and through his chosen prophet Joseph Smith, many important truths. One of those precious morsels of truth was that in some unspecified way, man has always existed. He taught us that there is indeed something called "intelligence, or the light of truth," which is an intrinsic part of that eternal existence (D&C 93:29). The scriptures and the living prophets further teach that man is literally a spiritually begotten child of God. These are revealed, known truths. The schools of thought discussed in this chapter are *man's attempts* through diligent scripture study and deep personal ponderings to reach a clearer understanding of the revealed doctrines. Inherent in those attempts, however, are limitations.

Elder Harold B. Lee in an address to religious educators cautioned against ascribing authority to any views that go beyond the revealed word.

> It is not to be thought that every word spoken by the General Authorities is inspired, or that they are moved upon by the Holy Ghost in everything they write. Now, you keep that in mind. I don't care what his position is, if he writes something or speaks something that goes beyond anything you can find in the standard Church works, unless that one be the prophet, seer, and revelator—please note that one exception—you may immediately say, "Well, that is his own idea."[18]

Amidst the questions and ponderings, it is wise to remember a caution given by President Joseph Fielding Smith. "Some of our writers have endeavored to explain what an intelligence is, but to do so is futile, for we have never been given any insight into this matter beyond what the Lord has fragmentarily revealed."[19]

This chapter has attempted to illustrate historically and doctrinally what is known and also what is not known on this subject. While it is wise to reserve final judgment on doctrines that have not been fully revealed, it is certainly permissible to ponder, question, and seek understanding and greater insight. As we do it, it is always better to be intellectually cautious, clinging to even fragmentary revealed truth rather than being superficially sure of "doctrines" that are based solely on logic, philosophy, or speculation. We may never know in this lifetime the specific role of intelligence in the eternal nature of man, but one thing we can know assuredly through scriptural insights, prophetic utterances, and personal revelation is that we are truly children of God.

Notes

1. Joseph Smith, *The Words of Joseph Smith*, compiled and edited by Andrew F. Ehat and Lyndon W. Cook (Provo, Utah: Religious Studies Center, Brigham Young University, 1980), p. 9; quoted from the "Willard Richards Pocket Companion," dated "before 8 August 1839."

2. Joseph Smith, *Teachings of the Prophet Joseph Smith*, (Salt Lake City: Deseret Book Co. 1972 [12th edition]), pp. 352–354.

3. Donald Q. Cannon and Larry E. Dahl, *The Prophet Joseph Smith's King Follett Discourse: A Six-Column Comparison of Original Notes and Amalgamations* (Provo, Utah: Religious Studies Center, Brigham Young University, 1983), pp. 48–53.

4. Blake Ostler, "The Idea of Pre-existence in the Development of Mormon Thought," *Dialogue: A Journal of Mormon Thought*, Spring 1982, pp. 59–78. See also Brigham Young's views as recorded in *Discourses of Brigham Young*, pp. 47–48. For another perspective of the historical development of this issue, see Kenneth W. Godfrey, "The History of Intelligence in Latter-day Saint Thought," unpublished paper presented at the 1988 Pearl of Great Price Symposium, Brigham Young University.

5. Parley P. Pratt, in *Journal of Discourses*, 1:8.

6. Charles W. Penrose, in *Journal of Discourses*, 26:23, 27; italics added.

7. Parley P. Pratt, *Key to the Science of Theology* (London: Latter-day Saints' Book Depot, 1855), pp. 43–45.

8. Joseph Fielding Smith, *The Progress of Man* (Salt Lake City: Deseret Book Co., 1964), p. 11; italics added.

9. Bruce R. McConkie, unpublished lecture transcript of Summer 1967 Seminary and Institute Teacher Seminar, Brigham Young University, in author's file. Audio tape of lecture is available in the BYU Religious Education Audiovisual Library.

10. Bruce R. McConkie, unpublished letter to Walter M. Horne, October 2, 1974. Photocopies of Mr. Horne's inquiry and Elder McConkie's reply are in author's file.

11. Orson Pratt, *The Seer* (Washington, D. C., 1855), p. 103.

12. The First Presidency, 1865, as quoted in *Messages of the First Presidency*, 6 vols. (Salt Lake City: Bookcraft, 1965), 2:233.

13. B. H. Roberts, *The Seventy's Course in Theology*, 4 vols. (Independence, Missouri: Zion's Printing and Publishing, 1907–1911), vol. 4 (1911), pp. 13–14. For a full examination of Elder Roberts's views on "intelligences," see also "Immortality of Man," *Improvement Era*, April 1907, pp. 403–423, and *The Seventy's Course in Theology*, vol. 4, lessons 1–5, pp. 1–23.

14. *Improvement Era*, April 1907, p. 403.

15. B. H. Roberts, "Immortality of Man," *Improvement Era*, April 1907, p. 406.

16. Bruce R. McConkie, Horne letter, p. 1.

17. Bruce R. McConkie, Horne letter, p. 5.

18. Harold B. Lee, "The Place of the Living Prophet, Seer, and Revelator," chapter 15 of *Stand Ye in Holy Places* (Salt Lake City: Deseret Book Co., 1974), pp. 162–63.

19. Joseph Fielding Smith, *The Progress of Man*, p. 11.

4

"I Am a Child of God"

The Lord revealed to the Prophet Joseph Smith many important truths concerning the Creation. One of those truths was that there were really two creations—one spiritual and the other temporal or physical. In the Doctrine and Covenants, the Lord said, "For by the power of my Spirit created I them; yea, all things both spiritual and temporal—first spiritual, secondly temporal" (D&C 29:31–32). Later, the Prophet Joseph was given additional information concerning these two creations. When he received the Lord's revelation given to Moses, Joseph learned that "the Lord God . . . created all things . . . spiritually, before they were naturally upon the face of the earth" (Moses 3:5). Concerning man, the Lord also said that even before Adam was created in the flesh, "all things [including mankind] were before created; but spiritually were they created and made according to my word" (Moses 3:7). To Adam, the Lord specifically stated, "I made the world, and men, before they were in the flesh" (Moses 6:51).

In the King Follett Discourse, Joseph Smith refuted the notion that God created the world *ex nihilo*—out of nothing— and explained that, instead, God organized the world.

> Now, I ask all who hear me, why the learned men who are preaching salvation, say that God created the heavens and the earth out of nothing? The reason is, that they are unlearned in the things of God, and have not the gift of the Holy Ghost. . . .
>
> You ask the learned doctors why they say the world was made out of nothing, and they will answer, "Doesn't the Bible say He *created* the world?" And they infer, from the word create, that it must have been made out of nothing. Now, the word create came from the word *baurau*, which does not mean to create out of nothing; it means to organize; the same as a man would organize materials and build a ship. Hence we infer that God had materials to organize the world out of chaos—chaotic matter, which is element, and in which dwells all the glory. Element had an existence from the time He had. The pure principles of element are principles which can never be destroyed; they may be organized and re-organized, but not destroyed. They had no beginning and can have no end.[1]

As previously discussed, the Prophet also taught that man was immortal, as is element. Was man organized out of "chaotic matter" as were God's other creations? The scriptures and inspired utterances of the prophets indicate clearly that there was a unique spiritual creation of man—different from all of God's other creations—wherein the immortal element or spirit matter was organized into a spirit being.

Man—the Spiritual Offspring of God

While speaking to ancient Athenian intellectuals about the unknown God whom they worshipped in ignorance, Paul told those gathered on Mars' hill that "we ought not to think that the Godhead is like unto gold, or silver, or stone, graven by art and man's device." Paul taught these philosophers that God was not an idol nor a creation of man's art or intellect, but rather a real, personal being "not far from every one of us." Paul knew the real nature of God because, as he stated, "we are the offspring of God" (Acts 17:27–29). Later, Paul reminded the Roman Saints of their unique relationship with God: "The Spirit itself beareth witness with our spirit, that we are the children of God" (Romans 8:16). To the Hebrew Saints, Paul gave another glimpse of man's spiritual origin when he referred to God as "the Father of spirits" (Hebrews 12:9).

The Prophet Joseph, in bearing witness of Christ and his creative role, distinguished between the spiritual creation or organization of all things in general and man specifically. He records, "We heard the voice bearing record that he [Jesus] is the Only Begotten of the Father—that by him, and through him, and of him, the worlds are and were created, and the inhabitants thereof are begotten sons and daughters unto God" (D&C 76:23–24).

With the restoration of the gospel and the priesthood keys through the Prophet there came also a renewed understanding of man's literal relationship to God. Every prophet in this dispensation has emphatically declared that man is truly a child of God.

Joseph Smith:

> The Spirit itself bears witness with our spirits that we are the children of God.[2]

Brigham Young:

> Our Father in Heaven begat all the spirits that ever were, or ever will be, upon this earth; and they were born spirits in the eternal world. Then the Lord by His power and wisdom organized the mortal tabernacle of man. We were made first spiritual, and afterwards temporal.[3]

John Taylor:

> Whence comest thou? Thine origin? What art thou doing here? . . . Knowest thou not that thou art a spark of Deity, struck from the fire of His eternal blaze, and brought forth in the midst of eternal burning?
>
> Knowest thou not that eternities ago thy spirit, pure and holy, dwelt in thy Heavenly Father's bosom and in His presence, and with thy mother, one of the queens of heaven, surrounded by thy brother and sister spirits in the spirit world, among the Gods?[4]

> "Our Father, who art in heaven." What, is He indeed my Father? Yes. Is He our Father? Yes. . . . We are children of God; that is the relationship we sustain to him.[5]

Wilford Woodruff:

> We know that we are created in the image of God, both male and female. . . .
>
> [God] is our Eternal Father.[6]

Lorenzo Snow:

> We believe that we are the offspring of our Father in heaven, and that we possess in our spiritual organizations the same capabilities, powers and faculties that our Father possesses. . . .
>
> We were born in the image of God our Father; he begot us like unto himself.[7]

Joseph F. Smith:

> Every spirit that comes to this earth to take upon it a tabernacle is a son or daughter of God and possesses all the intelligence and all the attributes that any son or daughter can enjoy.[8]

Heber J. Grant:

The doctrine of pre-existence pours a wonderful flood of light upon the otherwise mysterious problem of man's origin. It shows that man, as a spirit, was begotten and born of heavenly parents and reared to maturity in the eternal mansions of the Father, prior to coming upon the earth in a temporal body to undergo an experience in mortality.[9]

David O. McKay:

Man is a dual being—he is human, physical, of the earth, earthly, but he is, also, divine, the offspring of God.[10]

Joseph Fielding Smith:

We are informed that man was created in the image of God. . . . This is the answer to the evolutionist in relation to the descent of man, and to all religionists as well as scientists who ridicule the anthropomorphic nature of God. Man was created in the likeness of the body of God. We call him Father . . . he is literally the Father of the spirits of all men, and in the spirit they were created or begotten, sons and daughters unto him.[11]

Harold B. Lee:

Let us take a brief glimpse of our premortal life. . . . You were the sons and daughters of God in the pre-existent world of spirits. . . . Spirits are organized intelligences that were so prepared before the foundations of the earth were laid, and . . . they were organized by our Heavenly Father and dwelt with him while the earth was being formed. But now may I ask you a simple question: Could there have been a Father in heaven without a Mother? . . . If you consider carefully those in whose image and likeness male and female were created, I wonder if you will not also discover the organizers of intelligences in the world of spirits.[12]

Spencer W. Kimball:

> We are eternal beings. We have no way of comprehending how long we dwelt in the presence of God as his spirit children. . . .
>
> God made man in his own image and certainly he made woman in the image of his wife-partner. . . . You [women] are daughters of God. You are precious. You are made in the image of our heavenly Mother.[13]

Ezra Taft Benson:

> Knowledge is power, but the most vital and important knowledge is a knowledge of God—that he lives, that we are his children, that he loves us, that we are created in his image, that we can in faith pray to him and receive strength and inspiration in time of need. . . . But in all of our searching for truth, we must remember that the knowledge of our God, our Father, and his plans for us his children is of supreme importance.[14]

Implicit and explicit in each of these prophetic declarations are the words "offspring," "children," and "begotten." These words are fundamental to a precise understanding of the nature of the spiritual creation or organization of the spirits of mankind.

President Brigham Young taught that in order to better understand how to return to God's presence, it is imperative that we understand our relationship to the Eternal Father.

> The Scriptures which we believe have taught us from the beginning to call Him our Father, and we have been taught to pray to Him as our Father, in the name of our eldest brother whom we call Jesus Christ. . . . If I am not telling you the truth, please to tell me the truth on this subject, and let me know more than I do know. If it is hard for you to believe, . . . admit the fact as I state it, and do not contend against it. Try to believe it, because you will never become acquainted with our Father, never enjoy the blessings of His Spirit, never be prepared to enter into His pres-

ence, until you most assuredly believe . . . this great mystery about God.

What is this great mystery about God? Why do we call him Father? What does this mean about our spiritual origin? President Young continues:

> I want to tell you, each and every one of you, that you are well acquainted with God our heavenly Father, or the great Eloheim. You are all well acquainted with Him, for there is not a soul of you but what has lived in His house and dwelt with Him year after year. . . .
>
> There is not a person here to-day but what is a son or a daughter of that Being. In the spirit world their spirits were first begotten and brought forth, and they lived there with their parents for ages before they came here. This, perhaps, is hard for many to believe, but it is the greatest nonsense in the world not to believe it. If you do not believe it, cease to call Him Father; and when you pray, pray to some other character.[15]

A Heavenly Father and Mother

The First Presidency of the Church issued an official declaration concerning the spiritual as well as temporal origin of man. Presidents Joseph F. Smith, John R. Winder, and Anthon H. Lund wrote in 1909:

> All men and women are in the similitude of the universal Father and Mother, and are literally the sons and daughters of Deity. . . .
>
> The doctrine of the pre-existence—revealed so plainly, particularly in latter days, pours a wonderful flood of light upon the otherwise mysterious problem of man's origin. It shows that man, as a spirit, was begotten and born of heavenly parents, and reared to maturity in the eternal mansions of the Father, prior to coming upon the earth in a temporal body to undergo an experience in mortality. It teaches that all men existed in spirit before any man existed in the flesh,

and that all who have inhabited the earth since Adam have taken bodies and become souls in like manner. . . . Man is the child of God.[16]

It is interesting and significant to note the First Presidency's referral to both a Father and a Mother in heaven as literal parents of all of the spirits of mankind. It is most profound that they clarified the relationship of the spiritual creation of man by using words such as "begotten" and "born." This official statement of the First Presidency answers the question. How was the spirit of man organized or born? Just as mortal beings take on their physical bodies in a procreative process involving both an earthly father and an earthly mother, the birth of spirits came about "in like manner." This important truth implies that not only a Heavenly Father is needed in the spiritual procreative process but also a heavenly mother. It was this eternal logic that caused Eliza R. Snow in 1843 to write in her inspired hymn, "O My Father":

> In the heav'ns are parents single?
>   No, the thought makes reason stare!
> Truth is reason; truth eternal
>   Tells me I've a mother there.[17]

Other latter-day leaders of the Church have spoken concerning the role of both a Heavenly Father and Mother in this process of spirit birth. Elder Erastus Snow said:

Now, it is not said in so many words in the Scriptures, that we have a Mother in heaven as well as a Father. It is left for us to infer this from what we see and know of all living things in the *earth* including man. The male and female principle is united and both necessary to the accomplishment of the object of their being, and if this be not the case with our Father in heaven after whose image we are created, then it is an anomaly in nature. But to our minds the idea of a Father suggests that of a Mother. . . . Hence when it is said that God created our first parents in His likeness . . . it is intimated in language sufficiently plain to my understanding that the male and female principle was present with the Gods as it is with man.[18]

President Joseph Fielding Smith, in answering a question about a "Mother in Heaven," gave this response:

> In answer to your question about a mother in heaven, let us use reason. . . . If we had a Father, which we did, for all of these records speak of him, then does not good common sense tell us that we must have had a mother there also? . . .
>
> If we are his offspring, then how did we become such, if we had no mother to give us spirit birth? . . .
>
> Moreover, the Doctrine and Covenants definitely teaches the eternity of the marriage covenant and that those so married who are faithful will have claim on each other in eternity. Their children will belong to them, and they will have the gift of "a fulness and a continuation of the seeds forever and ever."[19]

As President Smith related, the latter-day revelations indicated that exalted men and women who have been faithful to the covenants of celestial marriage will have the opportunity to give birth to spiritual offspring. This part of the plan is no doubt patterned after that heavenly order which provided spirit bodies for all of mankind. Elder Orson Pratt commented on this pattern when he said:

> Before the earth was rolled into existence we were his sons and daughters. Those of his children who prove themselves during this probation worthy of exaltation in his presence, will beget other children, and, precisely according to the same principle, they too will become fathers of spirits, as he is the Father of our spirits; and thus the works of God are one eternal round—creation, glorification, and exaltation in the celestial kingdom.[20]

More recently Elder Bruce R. McConkie summarized the Church's teachings on the role of a heavenly mother in the spiritual creation of mankind and the relationship of this doctrine to the ultimate destiny of exalted men and women.

Implicit in the Christian verity that all men are the spirit children of an Eternal Father is the usually unspoken truth that they are also the offspring of an Eternal Mother. An exalted and glorified Man of Holiness (Moses 6:57) could not be a Father unless a Woman of like glory, perfection, and holiness was associated with him as a Mother. The begetting of children makes a man a father and a woman a mother whether we are dealing with man in his mortal or immortal state. . . .

Mortal persons who overcome all things and gain an ultimate exaltation will live eternally in the family unit and have spirit children, thus becoming Eternal Fathers and Eternal Mothers. (D&C 132:19–32.)[21]

Spiritual Capacities Inherited at Spirit Birth

Thus we see how closely our earthly existence is patterned after our premortal one. The similarities can be extended even further. Each child that is born into mortality inherits certain qualities and characteristics from his or her physical parents. Often a great athlete is referred to as a "born athlete" or it is said that he inherited certain gifts and skills from his parents or other progenitors. However, this inheritance can be more than just physical. It is also common to inherit musical talent, other artistic or intellectual gifts, and even personality traits. "It's in his blood" and "It's in her genes" are common expressions. In a real yet spiritual sense each child of Heavenly Father likewise inherited characteristics and capacities from his divine parents. These capacities may not necessarily be talents such as athletic ability or artistic gifts, but no doubt all spirit sons and daughters of God inherited the potential—all the spiritual capacities—necessary to enable them to become like their Father or Mother. "There is the nature of deity in the composition of our spiritual organization," said President Lorenzo Snow. "In our spiritual birth our Father transmitted to us the capabilities, powers and faculties which he himself possessed, as much so as the child on its mother's bosom possesses, although in an undeveloped state, the faculties, powers and susceptibilities of its parents."[22]

It should be significant to each of us to know that by virtue of our divine lineage, we possess innate spiritual capacities which, if developed and nurtured properly, will lead to godhood—godhood like that of the Father who endowed each of his spirit offspring with that inheritance. The key phrase used by President Snow was "although in an undeveloped state." This implies that though a spirit is endowed with inherited potential and spiritual capacities, they must still be faithfully developed. This principle is much the same in mortality. A person may be born with genetically endowed gifts or abilities, but if they remain undeveloped or unrefined that person will never rise to his or her potential. Each spirit child is truly a "god in embryo," but the development of that embryo is dependent upon continued spiritual growth and effort. President John Taylor, in 1892, elaborated on this concept in his classic work *The Mediation and Atonement*:

> If we take man, he is said to have been made in the image of God, for the simple reason that he is a son of God; and being His son, he is, of course, His offspring, an emanation from God, in whose likeness, we are told, he is made. He did not originate from a chaotic mass of matter, moving or inert, but came forth possessing, in an embryotic state, all the faculties and powers of a God. . . . As the horse, the ox, the sheep, and every living creature, including man, propagates its own species and perpetuates its own kind, so does God perpetuate His.[23]

Elder Orson Pratt explained it in this way:

> Will we ever become Gods? . . . In our imperfect state, being the children of God, we are destined, if we keep his commandments, to grow in intelligence until we finally become like God our Father. By living according to every word

which proceeds from the mouth of God, we shall attain to his likeness, the same as our children grow up and become like their parents; and, as children through diligence attain to the wisdom and knowledge of their parents, so may we attain to the knowledge of our Heavenly Parents.[24]

Spiritually Created in God's Image

Not only do we inherit spiritual potential from our Heavenly Father but also, according to numerous passages of scripture, we were created in the very image of God (see Genesis 1:26–27; Moses 2:26–27; Abraham 4:26–27; Mosiah 7:27; Ether 3:15). "In the day that God created man, in the likeness of God made he him; in the image of his own body, male and female, created he them" (Moses 6:8–9). These references to man's creation in the image of God's body apply just as much to the spirit bodies of mankind as to their physical bodies. The First Presidency's statement entitled "The Origin of Man" reiterates this principle.

> "God created man in His own image." This is just as true of the spirit as it is of the body, which is only the clothing of the spirit, its complement; the two together constituting the soul. The spirit of man is in the form of man, and the spirits of all creatures are in the likeness of their bodies. . . .
>
> Man is the child of God, formed in the divine image and endowed with divine attributes, and even as the infant son of an earthly father and mother is capable in due time of becoming a man, so the undeveloped offspring of celestial parentage is capable, by experience through ages and aeons, of evolving into a God.[25]

There are examples in the scriptures that illustrate this concept. When the premortal Christ appeared to the brother of Jared, he learned that the Savior's earthly body would be in the likeness of his spirit body.

> And the veil was taken from off the eyes of the brother of Jared, and he saw the finger of the Lord; and it was as the finger of a man, like unto flesh and blood. . . .

Seest thou that ye are created after mine own image? . . .

Behold, this body, which ye now behold, is the body of my spirit; and man have I created after the body of my spirit; and even as I appear unto thee to be in the spirit will I appear unto my people in the flesh. (Ether 3:6, 15–16.)

The Prophet Joseph Smith likewise learned through revelation from God that "that which is spiritual [is] in the likeness of that which is temporal; and that which is temporal in the likeness of that which is spiritual; the spirit of man in the likeness of his person" (D&C 77:2). The Prophet Joseph Smith further taught concerning not only the likeness of these premortal spirits but also the characteristics of spirit matter. "The spirit, by many, is thought to be immaterial, without substance. With this latter statement we should beg . . . to differ, and state the spirit is a substance; that it is material, but that it is more pure, elastic and refined matter than the body; that it existed before the body, can exist in the body; and will exist separate from the body, when the body will be mouldering in the dust; and will in the resurrection, be again united with it."[26]

Elder Parley P. Pratt explained that the spiritual elements were organized into a spirit being "in the likeness and after the pattern of the fleshly tabernacle. It [the spirit] possesses, in fact, all the organs and parts exactly corresponding to the outward tabernacle."[27]

Despite these scriptural examples and doctrinal teachings, there remain some questions regarding the nature of the premortal spirit of man. How closely does the spirit resemble the body? What about genetic or racial characteristics that are apparent in mankind's earthly bodies—were these also present in the premortal spirit bodies? We often see children in a family who look remarkably like each other or closely resemble a parent. What does this imply about our premortal relationships?

Elder Orson Pratt made some interesting comments pertaining to the resemblance between spirit and body. He said:

>We, as Latter-day Saints, believe that the spirits that oc-
>cupy these tabernacles have form and likeness *similar* to the
>human tabernacle. Of course there may be deformities exist-
>ing in connection with the outward tabernacle which do not
>exist in connection with the spirit that inhabits it. These
>tabernacles become deformed by accident in various ways,
>sometimes at birth, but this may not altogether or in any de-
>gree deform the spirits that dwell within them, therefore we
>believe that the spirits which occupy the bodies of the
>human family are *more or less in the resemblance of the tab-
>ernacles.*[28]

As Elder Pratt has pointed out, the revelations teach that
the spirits of mankind resemble their respective earthly
bodies generally rather than expressly. As a result, differences among peoples on earth such as racial distinctions, genetic imperfections, and inherited physical characteristics
may not be due to any differences in the spirits. President
David O. McKay said, in reference to the racial distinctions
among the peoples of the earth, "There were no national distinctions among those [premortal] spirits such as Americans,
Europeans, Asiatics, Australians, etc."[29] He further stated
that those distinctions came about only after these spirits entered their earthly existence. Similarly, the children in a
family who resemble each other or a parent closely do so because of the natural, biological laws of genetics rather than
by virtue of some premortal relationship, choice, or covenant. However, it must be emphasized that every person's
spirit was created literally in the image of God and that the
form and likeness of that spirit is due to divine parentage and
"spiritual genetics." What, then, does the spirit look like?
The answer is, like a child of God in the general form and
likeness of the physical body. Why, then, do the spirits of
men who leave mortality recognize the spirits of their de-
ceased family members or friends? There is no doubt that
spirits have the ability to recognize each other, both before
and after earth life; but that recognition is not due exclu-
sively to the earthly or physical characteristics of each person. Rather, spirits may also recognize others and be recog-

nized by others because of their spiritual relationships —associations as brothers and sisters, children of God.

So What?

Elder Boyd K. Packer wisely counselled all teachers of the gospel in his book *Teach Ye Diligently*, to apply the "So What?" test in their teaching of gospel principles. The "So What?" test involves imagining students of the gospel asking "So what?" regarding the principle or doctrine being taught. Nephi used this same principle when he taught his own people to "liken all scriptures" unto themselves (1 Nephi 19: 23). The Lord has revealed many important truths through his prophets concerning man's relationship to his Father in Heaven. No doubt the Lord had a greater purpose in mind when revealing these truths than merely answering intellectual or spiritual inquiry or settling doctrinal disputes. There are great blessings accompanying the revealed knowledge that we are literally children of God, endowed with his spiritual capacities and created in his image. These blessings include greater understanding of ourselves and our eternal destiny, renewed respect and reverence for ourselves, increased acceptance and understanding of God's dealings with his children, and greater confidence in and assurance of the existence of a caring, loving, and listening Father in Heaven. Having this knowledge of our literal relationship to God can profoundly enhance the esteem, reverence, and love in our three most important relationships—our relationships with self, others, and God.

Self-Respect

The Prophet Joseph Smith often said, "Would to God, brethren, I could tell you who I am."[30] Implicit in the Prophet's statement is an understanding that as literal children of

God there are significant things about our spiritual identity that may be hidden from view but that, if fully known, would heighten our self-respect and inspire us to a greater realization of our spiritual potential. This sense of heritage has certainly proven effective in mortality. Think, for instance of the deep pride and certitude of identity some feel in knowing that they have descended from famous noble ancestors; or think of the sense of purpose, duty, and belonging so often bred into those who bear the names of well-known and respected families. President Harold B. Lee, speaking in his last general conference, emphatically taught that an understanding of our relationship to God as literal spirit children can bring increased self-respect, which in turn leads us to greater righteousness and away from sin and despair.

> As I have prayerfully thought of the reasons why one chooses this course [of wickedness] . . . it seems to me that it all results from the failure of the individual to have self-respect. . . .
>
> . . . when one does not have that love for himself . . . other consequences can be expected to follow. He ceases to love life. Or if he marries, he has lost his love for his wife and children—no love of home or respect for the country in which he lives, and eventually he has lost his love of God. Rebellion in the land, disorder and the lack of love in the family, children disobedient to parents, loss of contact with God, all because that person has lost all respect for himself. . . .
>
> Well, then, "Who am I?" Those lacking in that important understanding, and, consequently, in some degree [those] failing to hold themselves in the high esteem which they would have if they did understand, are lacking self-respect. . . .
>
> . . . may I ask each of you again the question, "Who are you?" You are all sons and daughters of God. Your spirits were created and lived as organized intelligences before the world was. . . .
>
> If we can get a person to think what those words mean, then we can begin to understand the significance of the

words of the renowned psychologist, MacDougall, . . . "The first thing to be done to help a man to moral regeneration is to restore, if possible, his self-respect." How better may that self-respect be restored than to help him to fully understand the answer to that question, "Who am I?" . . .

What a difference it would make if we really sensed our divine relationship to God, our Heavenly Father, our relationship to Jesus Christ, our Savior and our elder brother, and our relationship to each other. . . .

Now . . . I trust that I might have given to you and others who have not yet listened to such counsel, something to stimulate some sober thinking as to who you are and from whence you came; and, in so doing, that I may have stirred up within your soul the determination to begin now to show an increased self-respect and reverence for the temple of God, your human body, wherein dwells a heavenly spirit. I would charge you to say again and again to yourselves . . . "I am a [son or daughter] of God" and by so doing, begin today to live closer to those ideals which will make your life happier and more fruitful because of an awakened realization of who you are.[31]

Our Father in Heaven has revealed through scriptures and prophets the fundamental truth that we are truly his children. This he has done to instill self-respect in the hearts of his children. President Thomas S. Monson has stated that by virtue of the increased self-respect that comes from this important knowledge, we also gain increased spiritual power to resist temptations, face life's adversities, and perform acts of righteousness, service, and charity.

To live greatly, we must develop the capacity to face trouble with courage, disappointment with cheerfulness, and triumph with humility. You ask, "How might we achieve these goals?" I answer, "By getting a true perspective of who we really are!" We are sons and daughters of a living God, in whose image we have been created. Think of that truth: "Created in the image of God." We cannot sincerely hold this conviction without experiencing a profound new sense of strength and power, even the strength to live the commandments of God, the power to resist the temptations of Satan.[32]

Knowing that we are literally children of God not only begets greater love and respect for ourselves but should also, logically, induce within us a stronger reverence and love for all mankind. Elder Boyd K. Packer asked, "What could inspire one to purity and worthiness more than to possess a spiritual confirmation that we are the children of God? What could inspire a more lofty regard for oneself, or engender more love for mankind?"[33]

Universal Brotherhood

Knowing that all men are the offspring of God also means knowing that all mankind are literally spiritual brothers and sisters. This universal brotherhood is not merely a symbolic or literary dictum but rather a spiritually significant reality. Just as a knowledge of our celestial lineage can positively affect our self-esteem and personal behavior, so does it affect our attitude of love and our actions of service toward our fellowmen—our brothers and sisters. Universal brotherhood is more than just world citizenship; it truly is a divine family relationship. As George Bernard Shaw is quoted as writing: "If we all realized that we were the children of one father, we would stop shouting at each other as much as we do."[34]

There Is a God in Heaven: He Is My Father

This knowledge of God not only builds self-respect, a greater desire to be righteous, and stronger feelings of universal brotherhood but also, most important, it teaches us that there really is a God in Heaven who is truly and literally our loving and caring Father. Understanding his nature and our relationship to him builds our faith and can bring us to a more meaningful communication with him. President David O. McKay once said, "A belief in God brings peace to the soul. An assurance that God is our Father, into whose presence we can go for comfort and guidance, is a never-failing source of comfort."[35]

Because we find it easier to commune with such a God, we can attain greater spirituality, firmer faith, more resolute repentance, and a stronger commitment to fulfill our spiritual destiny. As we grow in these things, we gain a clearer understanding of the Father's plan for his children. Elder Boyd K. Packer spoke of the blessing of understanding that comes from an enlightened and enhanced relationship with the Father of all spirits.

> When we understand the doctrine of premortal life, then things fit together and make sense. We then know that little boys and little girls are not monkeys, nor are their parents, nor were theirs, to the very beginning generation.
>
> We are the children of God, created in his image.
>
> Our child-parent relationship to God is clear.
>
> The purpose for the creation . . . is clear.
>
> The testing that comes in mortality is clear.
>
> The need for a redeemer is clear.
>
> When we do understand that principle of the gospel, we see a Heavenly Father and a Son; we see an atonement and a redemption.[36]

Many people become discouraged in their quest to know God, finding him incomprehensible and impersonal. Such confusion often creates spiritual roadblocks to personal prayer. It is not uncommon for one lacking this knowledge to feel that God does not really know him or listen to his prayers. With this discouragement, he often ceases to communicate with God and thus further estranges himself from his Father. On the other hand, knowing that he is truly the child of a personal God—spiritually begotten of Him and created in His image—brings him a clearer vision of the type of being that God is, and thus brings him closer to his heavenly parent. Elder Bruce R. McConkie stated that understanding God comes hand in hand with the knowledge of our personal relationship to him.

> How can we conceive of such an Omnipotent God? How can mere man ever hope to know him whom it is eternal life to know? Can man comprehend God?
>
> Strangely, marvelously, wondrously, the answer is found in the simple declaration that God is our Father. Our finite minds cannot comprehend his infinite laws. But we can envision him as a Father, as a personal, loving being filled with tenderness and compassion. He is more than the Father of the Firstborn; more than the Father of the Only Begotten in the flesh; more than the Father in the sense that he created the first mortal man. He is, in deed and in fact, the Father of the spirits of all men in the literal and full sense of the word. Each of us was begotten by him in the premortal life. We are his spirit children.[37]

Knowing that all men everywhere are in reality the spiritual children of God, created in his image, endowed with his characteristics and capacities, gives rise not only to increased knowledge but also to enhanced respect and reverence for self, fellowmen, and God. The words of the familiar Primary song "I Am a Child of God" may be simple, but they are profound.

> I am a child of God.
> Rich blessings are in store;
> If I but learn to do his will
> I'll live with him once more.
>
> Lead me, guide me, walk beside me,
> Help me find the way.
> Teach me all that I must do
> To live with him someday.[38]

There is a message of hope and inspiration in that simple, familiar refrain. The Lord has revealed this knowledge as motivation to his children to live in such a way that they might return to their heavenly home. Someday, as Brigham Young foresaw, there will be a happy homecoming reunion with our Heavenly Father.

> He is the Father of our spirits; and if we could know, understand, and do His will, every soul would be prepared to return back into His presence. And when they get there, they would see that they had formerly lived there for ages, that they had previously been acquainted with every nook and corner, with the palaces, walks, and gardens; and they would embrace their Father, and He would embrace them and say, "My son, my daughter, I have you again;" and the child would say, "O my Father, my Father, I am here again."[39]

Notes

1. Joseph Smith, *History of the Church* (Salt Lake City: Deseret Book Co., 1967), 6:308–309.

2. Joseph Smith, *The Words of Joseph Smith*, compiled by Andrew F. Ehat and Lyndon W. Cook (Salt Lake City: Religious Studies Center, Brigham Young University, 1980), p. 382. This statement of the Prophet was recorded in the George Laub journal on 16 June 1844.

3. Brigham Young, in *Journal of Discourses*, 1:50.

4. John Taylor, "The Mormon," as cited in Daniel H. Ludlow, comp., *Latter-day Prophets Speak* (Salt Lake City: Bookcraft, 1951), p. 8.

5. John Taylor, in *Journal of Discourses*, 24:2–3.

6. Wilford Woodruff, in *Journal of Discourses*, 18:32; 24:53.

7. Lorenzo Snow, in *Journal of Discourses*, 14:300, 302.

8. Joseph F. Smith, in *Young Women's Journal*, 6:371–372.

9. Heber J. Grant, in *Improvement Era*, September 1925, p. 1090.

10. David O. McKay, *Treasures of Life* (Salt Lake City: Deseret Book Co., 1962), p. 413.

11. Joseph Fielding Smith, *Man: His Origin and Destiny* (Salt Lake City: Deseret Book Co., 1954), p. 268.

12. Harold B. Lee, *Youth and the Church* (Salt Lake City: Deseret Book Co., 1953), pp. 123–125.

13. Spencer W. Kimball, *The Teachings of Spencer W. Kimball*, Edward L. Kimball, ed. (Salt Lake City: Bookcraft, 1982), pp. 24–25.

14. Ezra Taft Benson, *God, Family, Country: Our Three Great Loyalties* (Salt Lake City: Deseret Book Co., 1974), p. 1.

15. Brigham Young, in *Journal of Discourses*, 4:216.

16. The First Presidency (Joseph F. Smith, John R. Winder, Anthon H. Lund) "The Origin of Man," *Improvement Era*, November 1909, pp. 75–81. Reprinted in James R. Clark, comp., *Messages of the First Presidency*, 6 vols. (Salt Lake City: Bookcraft, 1965), 4:203, 205, 206.

17. Eliza R. Snow, "O My Father," *Hymns*, no. 292.

18. Erastus Snow, in *Journal of Discourses*, 26:214.

19. Joseph Fielding Smith, *Answers to Gospel Questions* (Salt Lake City: Deseret Book Co., 1972), 3:142–144.

20. Orson Pratt, in *Journal of Discourses*, 18:293.

21. Bruce R. McConkie, *Mormon Doctrine*, 2nd edition (Salt Lake City: Bookcraft, 1966), pp. 516–517.

22. Lorenzo Snow, in *Journal of Discourses*, 14:302.

23. John Taylor, *The Mediation and Atonement* (Salt Lake City: Deseret News Co., 1882), pp. 164–165.

24. Orson Pratt, in *Journal of Discourses*, 18:292.

25. The First Presidency, "The Origin of Man," *Improvement Era*, November, 1909, p. 77.

26. Joseph Smith, *Teachings of the Prophet Joseph Smith* (Salt Lake City: Deseret Book Co., 1972), p. 207.

27. Parley P. Pratt, *Key to the Science of Theology* (Salt Lake City: Deseret Book Co., 1979), p. 79.

28. Orson Pratt, in *Journal of Discourses*, 15:242–243.

29. David O. McKay, *Home Memories of President David O. McKay*, compiled by Llewelyn R. McKay (Salt Lake City: Deseret Book Co., 1956), p. 228.

30. Joseph Smith, quoted in Orson F. Whitney, *Life of Heber C. Kimball* (Salt Lake City: Bookcraft, 1945), p. 322.

31. Harold B. Lee, "Understanding Who We Are Brings Self-Respect," *Ensign*, January 1974, pp. 2–6.

32. Thomas S. Monson, in Conference Report, April 1973, p. 62.

33. Boyd K. Packer, Conference Report, October 1984, p. 85.

34. George Bernard Shaw, as quoted by Harold B. Lee, *Ensign*, January 1974, p. 6.

35. David O. McKay, *Secrets of Happy Life*, compiled by Llewelyn R. McKay (Salt Lake City: Bookcraft, 1967), p. 114.

36. Boyd K. Packer, in Conference Report, October 1983, p. 22.

37. Bruce R. McConkie, *A New Witness for the Articles of Faith* (Salt Lake City: Deseret Book Co., 1985), pp. 61–62.

38. "I Am a Child of God" *Hymns*, no. 301.

39. Brigham Young, in *Journal of Discourses*, 4:268.

5

What Was It Like?

Questions often arise regarding the conditions that prevailed in the premortal existence. What was it like? Did it look much different than this world? What did spirits do there? Was there sin and opposition there? How long were we there? How much did we know about earth life and what to expect here? These and many other questions cannot be fully answered, because the Lord has not seen fit to reveal many of the details of our premortal home. He has, however, revealed through the scriptures and through his latter-day prophets some important information that sheds significant doctrinal light on the general conditions in the premortal life. Much of what is known about these conditions is learned indirectly, by inference from scriptural passages about important gospel principles and by transferring and applying that knowledge to the premortal realm. For example, we can gain some insights by examining the teachings of the scriptures on related issues such as the War in Heaven, agency, progression, and the postmortal spirit world. This chapter will examine the doctrinal teachings concerning premortal conditions and will also make appropriate inferences and assumptions when they can be supported by revelations and teachings of the prophets. Specific questions may remain unanswered, but the scriptures and prophets have given enough inspired information to help us understand the general, fundamental conditions of the premortal world.

God's House Is a House of Order

Numerous scriptural passages set forth an important principle of God's house, both heavenly and earthly, as being order. God's house is a house of order (see D&C 132:8). The Lord also speaks of the order that prevails in his heavenly and earthly houses as "everlasting order" (D&C 82:20). His counsel to his earthly servants reflects the order and harmony that must also have prevailed in his house where his premortal offspring dwelt with him. In establishing his latter-day Church, the Lord said that it was essential "that all things . . . be done in order" (D&C 20:68). The order that prevailed in the premortal home can be seen in the three main ways—organization, priesthood, and instruction.

Organization

From scripture and prophetic utterance we can learn that there was organization in the premortal world. Such organization was designed to most effectively meet the Father's objectives of instruction and preparation of his children. It would not be unreasonable, then, to think that the following counsel and charge from the Lord to his latter-day servants was in fact similar to or based upon the premortal charge of the Father to his spirit children to prepare themselves for their earthly ministry and experience.

Assemble yourselves together, and organize yourselves, and prepare yourselves . . . that you shall teach one another the doctrine of the kingdom.

Teach ye diligently and my grace shall attend you, that you may be instructed more perfectly in theory, in principle, in doctrine, in the law of the gospel, in all things that pertain unto the kingdom of God . . .

That ye may be prepared in all things when I shall send you again to magnify the calling whereunto I have called you, and the mission with which I have commissioned you. (D&C 88:74, 77–78, 80.)

In speaking of the Creation, the Lord revealed that "that which is temporal [is] in the likeness of that which is spiritual" (D&C 77:2). Could this passage also have a broader meaning which may indeed apply to spiritual organizations and orders that serve as the pattern for the temporal or earthly? In light of this musing, it is interesting to compare the Lord's pattern for his earthly house with the conditions that may have existed in his heavenly house. He said, "Organize yourselves; prepare every needful thing; and establish a house, even a house of prayer, a house of fasting, a house of faith, a house of learning, a house of glory, a house of order, a house of God" (D&C 88:119).

President Brigham Young reported that some time after the Prophet Joseph Smith's death, the Prophet Joseph returned to Brigham and instructed him, giving him certain counsels to be shared with the Saints. Joseph then told Brigham to "be sure to tell the people to keep the spirit of the Lord; and if they will, they will find themselves just as they were organized by our Father in Heaven before they came into the world. Our father in Heaven organized the human family, but they are all disorganized and in great confusion."[1]

The Prophet Joseph Smith counseled the Saints to live the gospel and stay in tune with the Spirit and they would eventually find themselves organized in the perfect order and union of God as they were before this life. It may be possible to gain a glimpse of that premortal order and organization by understanding better the organization God provides for his children both in this life and in the post-earth spirit world. While Joseph referred to a future organization and order patterned after the premortal order, President Heber C. Kimball recounted a vision of Jedediah M. Grant of the order and organization in the post-earth spirit world. It is interesting to note how his description might apply to a similar premortal house of order.

> He said to me, "Brother Heber, I have been into the spirit world two nights in succession, and, of all the dreads that ever came across me, the worst was to have to again return to my body, though I had to do it. But O," says he, "the order and government that were there! When in the spirit world, I saw the order of righteous men and women; beheld them organized in their several grades, and there appeared to be no obstruction to my vision; I could see every man and woman in their grade and order. I looked to see whether there was any disorder there, but there was none; neither . . . darkness, disorder or confusion." . . . All were organized and in perfect harmony.[2]

Wherever the kingdom of God exists—premortally, on earth, and postmortally—there have been order and organization, priesthood keys, offices, and assignments. While it is not fully clear how the premortal world was organized, there is ample evidence to show that there were councils organized to instruct, plan, prepare, and make important decisions for the implementation of the plan of salvation. As with the kingdom of God on earth, the order and organization of heaven is everlastingly intertwined with priesthood. President Joseph Fielding Smith illustrated how all things were done in order and organization under the direction of God's eternal power.

> There must be leaders, presiding officers, and those who are worthy and able to take command. During the ages in which we dwelt in the pre-mortal state we not only developed our various characteristics and showed our worthiness

and ability, or the lack of it, but we were also where such progress could be observed. It is reasonable to believe that there was a Church organization there. The heavenly beings were living in a perfectly arranged society. Every person knew his place. Priesthood, without any question, had been conferred and the leaders were chosen to officiate. Ordinances pertaining to that pre-existence were required and the love of God prevailed.[3]

Priesthood in the Premortal Life

The prophet Alma spoke of "those priests [who] were ordained after the order of his Son. . . . And this is the manner after which they were ordained—being called and prepared from the foundation of the world." (Alma 13:2–3.) Prophets of the Restoration have declared, as did Alma of old, that priesthood authority and organization existed in the premortal courts of the Father. The Prophet Joseph Smith stated:

> The Priesthood is an everlasting principle, and existed with God from eternity, and will to eternity, without beginning of days or end of years. The keys have to be brought from heaven whenever the Gospel is sent. . . .
> . . . [The Melchizedek Priesthood] holds the highest authority which pertains to the priesthood, and the keys of the Kingdom of God in all ages of the world to the latest posterity on the earth; and is the channel through which all knowledge, doctrine, the plan of salvation and every important matter is revealed from heaven.
> Its institution was prior to "the foundation of this earth."[4]

The Prophet clearly states that priesthood is eternal and that through that eternal channel comes the knowledge and instruction necessary to prepare the spirit children of God for eventual exaltation. This pattern of priesthood instruction applies to the premortal life as well as to this life and to the postmortal world of the spirits.

Counselling men of the priesthood, President Wilford Woodruff said: "I feel that we should humble ourselves before God, that we should labor to magnify our callings, and honor this priesthood which we received before we came here."[5]

President Joseph Fielding Smith further declared, "In regard to the holding of the priesthood in pre-existence, I will say that there was an organization there just as well as an organization here, and men there held authority. Men chosen to positions of trust in the [premortal] spirit world held priesthood."[6]

Priesthood, then, as the power of God, was the basis for the order and organization of the premortal heavenly home. It is truly the "perfect system of government" described by President Brigham Young.[7] President John Taylor also commented on the role of priesthood in the premortal organization of heaven.

> What is priesthood? Without circumlocution, I shall briefly answer that it is the government of God, whether on earth or in the heavens, for it is by that power, agency, or principle that all things are governed on earth and in the heavens, and by that power all things are upheld and sustained. It governs all things—it directs all things—it sustains all things—and has to do with all things that God and truth are associated with. It is the power of God delegated to intelligences in the heavens and to men on the earth; and when we arrive in the celestial kingdom of God, we shall find the most perfect order and harmony existing, because there is the perfect pattern, the most perfect order of government.[8]

The premortal home was, indeed, the celestial kingdom for our heavenly parents. No doubt, its priesthood organization and order was the pattern for all other councils and organizations designed to bring about God's purposes. President Ezra Taft Benson has taught that councils organized under the priesthood authority play an important role in Church government in "correlating, coordinating, planning, and resolving." Quoting Stephen L Richards, President Benson continued, "As I conceive it, the genius of our Church government is government through *councils*. . . . I have had enough experiences to know the value of councils. . . . I see the wisdom, God's wisdom, in creating councils . . . to govern his Kingdom."[9]

The scriptures also refer to a premortal council. The plan of salvation and its attendant laws and principles were "ordained in the midst of the Council of the Eternal God of all other gods before this world was" (D&C 121:32). Abraham also saw in vision that prior to the formation of the earth, "the Gods took counsel among themselves" (Abraham 4:26).

Many of the latter-day prophets have referred to the preparations that took place in the premortal Grand Council. The Prophet Joseph Smith said, "At the first organization in heaven we were all present, and saw the Savior chosen and appointed and the plan of salvation made, and we sanctioned it."[10] No doubt instruction was a primary purpose of the Grand Council. The spirits were once again taught the principles of the plan of salvation, the need for a Savior, and the blessings of the Atonement. President Joseph F. Smith also stated that the spirits of all men were also present at other times when the plans were presented and the principles taught.

> Our spirits existed before they came to this world. They were in the councils of the heavens before the foundations of the earth were laid. . . . We sang together with the heavenly hosts for joy, when the foundations of the earth were laid, and when the plan of our existence upon this earth and redemption were mapped out. . . . We were unquestionably present in those councils. . . . We were, no doubt, there, and took a part in all those scenes; we were vitally concerned in the carrying out of these great plans and purposes; we understood them, and it was for our sakes they were decreed and are to be consummated.[11]

It is interesting to note that President Smith used the plural term "councils," which implies that there were perhaps many councils, in addition to the Grand Council. These many councils, functioning under priesthood direction, were a time for organization and preparation and for formal instruction and counsel which led us to greater understanding of the laws of God, the role of mortality in the plan of salvation, and any other principle designed to "bring to pass the immortality and eternal life of man" (Moses 1:39). It might be appropriate to compare these premortal councils to latter-day general conferences—formal meetings to instruct, to edify, and to "do whatever church business is necessary" (D&C 20:62).

Instruction

Lehi taught his son Jacob that in order for men to be able to "choose liberty and eternal life, through the great Mediator of all men, or to choose captivity and death" (2 Nephi 2:27) they must be "instructed sufficiently that they know good from evil. And the law is given unto men." (2 Nephi 2:5.) Alma wrote that those priests "after the order of [God's] son" who were foreordained in the premortal world had been "prepared from the foundation of the world" (Alma 13:2–3). No doubt the premortal preparation process included instruction and diligence much the same as mortal priesthood preparation. Alma also states that those foreordained priests were called "*to teach* his commandments unto the children of men" (Alma 13:6; italics added). Although Alma is specifically referring to their earthly priesthood service, teaching the gospel was surely a central part of their premortal priesthood assignments as well.

President Joseph F. Smith learned in his vision of the redemption of the dead (D&C 138) that some were "the noble and great ones who were chosen in the beginning to be rulers in the Church of God. Even before they were born they, with many others, received their first lessons in the world of spirits and were prepared to come forth in . . . due time."

(D&C 138:55–56.) These "first lessons" were administered in God's premortal house of order and organization in much the same way as the gospel is taught and the work of God is overseen in mortality.

Just as modern-day general conferences or councils are not the exclusive means of instructing the Saints, neither were the premortal councils. It is logical to assume that there was much informal instruction in gospel laws and principles in addition to instruction in the formal councils. In the 1909 First Presidency statement entitled "The Origin of Man," it is stated that "man, as a spirit, was begotten and born of heavenly parents, and reared to maturity in the eternal mansions of the Father."[12] As discussed in an earlier chapter, this statement certainly applies to the maturing of the actual spirit personage, but it is also logical to assume that the word *reared* has a broader meaning as well. Just as, in mortality, rearing by loving, caring parents means infinitely more than merely watching the child grow in physical stature, so it seems to imply more in relationship to a premortal upbringing. While not explicitly stated, it could well be that one of the primary purposes for the extended stay of spirits in the premortal world was that they might be taught and prepared in all necessary ways—by instruction, observation, and experience—for their mortal sojourn.

A House of Agency

The scriptures show clearly that one of the fundamental conditions in the premortal existence for all of the Father's spirit children was that of agency. Agency is an eternal principle and essential to the entire plan of salvation. In one of the most profound, consequential decisions of all eternity, the spirit offspring of God exercised this agency as they chose either to follow the plan of salvation outlined by the Father, with Christ as the Savior, or to reject that plan and follow

Lucifer in premortal rebellion (see D&C 29:36–37; Moses 4:3). Since the children of God exercised their agency in choosing to follow Christ or to rebel with Lucifer, it is also logical to infer from the scriptures that the premortal spirits exercised their agency in myriad other ways. In fact, their use of agency, as evidenced by their choice of Christ or Lucifer and their level of commitment to that choice, was the result of many other previous choices made by virtue of that agency.

Knowing that men exercised agency in the premortal world can tell us something about other premortal conditions. Certain circumstances must have prevailed in order to effect this freedom of choice. Elder Bruce R. McConkie wrote that four fundamental principles must always exist for agency to operate.

> Four great principles must be in force if there is to be agency: 1. Laws must exist, laws ordained by an Omnipotent power, laws which can be obeyed or disobeyed; 2. Opposites must exist—good and evil, virtue and vice, right and wrong —that is, there must be an opposition, one force pulling one way and another pulling the other; 3. A knowledge of good and evil must be had by those who are to enjoy the agency, that is, they must know the difference between the opposites; and 4. An unfettered power of choice must prevail.[13]

Laws

As previously mentioned, part of the order and organization of the premortal house of God was the establishment of laws—the eternal laws and the principles of the plan of redemption. We know these laws were in force in premortal realms because the Lord taught the Prophet Joseph Smith concerning "all covenants, contracts, bonds, obligations, oaths, vows, performances, connections, associations, or expectations" that are part of the "new and everlasting covenant" of the restored gospel: "For all who will have a blessing at my hands shall abide the *law* which was appointed for that blessing, and the conditions thereof, *as were instituted from before the foundation of the world.* . . . Will I accept of an offering, saith the Lord, that is not made in my name? Or will I receive at your hands that which I have not appointed? And will I appoint unto you, saith the Lord, except it be by law, even as I and my Father ordained unto you, *before the world was?*" (D&C 132:4, 5, 7, 9–11, italics added; see also D&C 130:20–21.) Later in the same revelation, Joseph was told that the Lord would give to the Saints "the law of my Holy Priesthood, as was ordained by me and my Father before the world was" (D&C 132:28). Earlier the Lord had commanded Joseph to build a temple "that those ordinances might be revealed which had been hid from before the world was. . . . For I deign to reveal unto my church things which have been kept hid from before the foundation of the world." (D&C 124:38, 41.) The Prophet Joseph Smith clearly taught that the laws, principles, and ordinances of the gospel were ordained and established *before the earth came into existence.*

> It was the design of the councils of heaven before the world was, that the principles and laws of the priesthood should be predicated upon the gathering of the people in every age of the world. . . . Ordinances instituted in the heavens before the foundation of the world, in the priesthood, for the salvation of men, are not to be altered or changed. All must be saved on the same principles. . . .
>
> . . . Could you gaze into heaven five minutes, you would know more than you would by reading all that ever was written on the subject.
>
> We are only capable of comprehending that certain things exist, which we may acquire by certain fixed principles. If men would acquire salvation, they have got to be subject, before they leave this world, to certain rules and principles, which were fixed by an unalterable decree before the world was. . . .
>
> The organization of the spiritual and heavenly worlds, and of spiritual and heavenly beings, was agreeable to the

most perfect order and harmony: their limits and bounds were fixed irrevocably, and voluntarily subscribed to in their heavenly estate by themselves, and were by our first parents subscribed to upon the earth. Hence the importance of embracing and subscribing to principles of eternal truth by all men upon the earth that expect eternal life.[14]

Jacob taught the necessity of these laws and principles when he said, "Wherefore, he has given a law; and where there is no law given there is no punishment; and where there is no punishment there is no condemnation" (2 Nephi 9:25). In order for the plan of salvation to be operative, there must be laws established and taught to the children of God. The premortal councils ensured that all were instructed sufficiently in the laws in order that they might be able to use their agency to choose wisely.

Opposition

Lehi taught his son Jacob "that there is an opposition in all things. If not so . . . righteousness could not be brought to pass" (2 Nephi 2:11). In order for agency to operate in the premortal world, as well as on earth, there was a need for opposites, otherwise, "man could not act for himself save it should be that he was enticed by the one or the other" (2 Nephi 2:16). This is as much an eternal verity as is agency. "What can you know except by its opposite?" queried Brigham Young. "Who could number the days, if there were no nights to divide the day from the night? Angels could not enjoy the blessings of light eternal, were there no darkness. All that are exalted and all that will be exalted will be exalted upon this principle. . . . No person, either in heaven or upon earth, can enjoy and understand these things upon any other principle."[15]

Opposition is more than merely good and evil or virtue and vice. Sin and righteousness, which surely did exist there, are only two of numerous examples. Just as there is a variety of opposition in mortality, so it was in the premortal home. Not all choices were merely between good and evil, but all contributed to our schooling in the use of our agency.

Knowledge of Good and Evil

Closely associated with the principle of opposition is the necessity for men to know the difference between opposites. In the premortal world, this knowledge came in two ways—by instruction and by experience. Not only were our fledgling spirits tutored in gospel principles and a cognitive knowledge of good and evil but also consequences for choices were clearly laid out. Complete understanding of good and evil could not be obtained by instruction alone. The capstone of this knowledge was gained by virtue of experience—by making choices between the opposites and by experiencing the consequences for those choices. The premortal experience of good and evil was limited, however. We could not, as spirits, experience all aspects of righteousness and wickedness. Some things could only be learned and experienced with physical bodies in a temporal world. We did, nevertheless, gain knowledge in our premortal home of good and evil by effective instruction coupled with important, though limited, experience.

Unfettered Power of Choice

The great Lamanite prophet Samuel taught the relationship between knowledge of good and evil and the freedom to choose when he said, "Ye are free; ye are permitted to act for yourselves; for behold, God hath given unto you a knowledge and he hath made you free. He hath given unto you that ye might know good from evil, and he hath given unto you that ye might choose life or death; and ye can do good and be restored unto that which is good . . . or ye can do evil, and have that which is evil restored unto you." (Helaman 14:30–31.)

This freedom of choice operated in much the same way premortally as it does here on earth. Agency could not fully function if the Father did not allow his children the freedom to make choices based on the principles of law, opposites, and knowledge of good and evil. Man must not be compelled in any way, but conditions must exist in which he could make his own choices and be held accountable. These four principles required for the operation of agency can best be understood by looking at the results of the exercise of agency in the premortal life.

Various Levels of Righteousness and Progression

Because of individual agency and accountability there has always been diversity among the children of God—varying levels of obedience, faithfulness, service, and devotion; differing degrees of understanding and acceptance of and adherence to gospel principles. Because infinite possibilities of right and wrong and greater and lesser choices exist, individual agency produces great differences among the children of God. The scriptures give examples of the differences among spirits. Abraham saw in vision the premortal children of God. He saw the various spirits and observed that they were not equally intelligent (see Abraham 3:18–19). "Now the Lord had shown unto me, Abraham, the intelligences that were organized before the world was; and among all these there were many of the noble and great ones; And God saw these souls that they were good" (Abraham 3:22–23).

Implicit in Abraham's description of the premortal spirit world is the fact that not all of the spirits were among "the noble and great ones," and neither were all of the spirit children of God equally worthy of the appellation "good." Their differences were due to the eternal principle of agency. President Brigham Young stated that just as there are vast differences between men on earth, there are likewise differences among spirits.

> Can any man tell the variety of the spirits there are? No, he cannot even tell the variety that there is in the portion of his dominions in which God has placed us, on this earth upon which we live. . . . You may observe the people, and you will see an endless variety of disposition. . . . Where can you point out two precisely alike in every particular in their temperaments and dispositions? Where can you find two who are so operated upon precisely alike by a superior power that their lives, their actions, their feelings . . . are alike? I conclude that there is as great a variety in the spiritual as there is in the temporal world.[16]

The prophet Alma, in speaking of those high priests who had received the priesthood before their mortal birth, identified some of the reasons for their selection and their higher level of progression. They were "called and prepared from the foundation of the world according to the foreknowledge of God, on account of their exceeding faith and good works; in the *first place* being left to choose good or evil; therefore they *having chosen good, and exercising exceedingly great faith,* are called with a holy calling" (Alma 13:3–4; italics added). President Joseph Fielding Smith also stated that individual agency led to different levels of obedience, diligence, and righteousness, which, in turn, resulted in varying levels of progression, of capacities, and ultimately of authority and responsibility.

> God gave his children their free agency even in the spirit world, by which the individual spirits had the privilege, just as men have here, of choosing the good and rejecting the evil, or partaking of the evil to suffer the consequences of their sins. Because of this, some even there were more faithful than others in keeping the commandments of the Lord. Some were of greater intelligence than others, as we find it here, and were honored accordingly. . . .
>
> The spirits of men had their free agency, some were greater than others. . . . The spirits of men were not equal.

They may have had an equal start, and we know they were all innocent in the beginning; but the right of free agency which was given to them enabled some to outstrip others, and thus, through the eons of immortal existence, to become more intelligent, more faithful, for they were free to act for themselves, to think for themselves, to receive the truth or rebel against it.[17]

The Effects of Opposition in the Premortal Life

Note in the previous statement from President Joseph Fielding Smith the phrases "just as men have here" and "as we find it here." From these phrases and the scriptural references already cited, we can infer that the premortal spirits had opportunities and requirements to be obedient, diligent, and faithful as do mortals on earth. They were expected to study and learn, as previously discussed. They were expected to be faithful in whatever commandments and duties the Father required of them. They were to develop talents, skills, and abilities that would enable them to live more productive and fulfilling lives, both there and here. They were to show love, kindness, patience, and consideration to their brothers and sisters. Each of these expectations is the same "as we find it here." Whatever other specific expectations and requirements existed there is not revealed. It certainly is logical to assume, however, that premortal spirits were expected to live the same gospel principles, with the exception of earthly ordinances, as men in the flesh. Scriptural passages such as Alma 13:3–4 seem to indicate that they exercised faith in Christ and the plan of redemption and repented there as men do here.

Since there must be opposition in order for agency to operate fully and since there was premortal goodness, there was also premortal wickedness. If there was premortal diligence and faithfulness, there must also have been premortal sloth-fulness, laziness, and disobedience just as there is in men here. For, as Lehi explains, "it must needs be that there was an opposition. . . . Wherefore, the Lord God gave unto man that he should act for himself. Wherefore, man could not act for himself save it should be that he was enticed by the one or the other." (2 Nephi 2:15–16.)

Undoubtedly, then, sin was possible because of agency and because of the enticements of opposition. The scriptures indicate that there were not only a variety of sins of omission, such as failure to be as faithful or as diligent as possible, but also sins of commission, such as Lucifer's blatant rebellion. Some have attempted to portray the premortal home as a glorious celestial kingdom wherein no unclean thing can dwell, where there is only goodness, righteousness, and obedience—a place in the constant presence of God where the spirits would have no desire or outlet for anything less than celestial thoughts or actions.[18] Such a view would not allow for an unfettered power of choice, or for the need for faith and continual diligence, and would eliminate the diversity among the spirits. Under such illogical conditions, how would some be "noble and great," and yet not all? Orson Pratt asked this question: "If all the two-thirds who kept their first estate were equally valiant in the war, and equally faithful, why should some of them be called and chosen in their spiritual state to hold responsible stations and offices in this world, while others were not? If there were none of those spirits who sinned, why were the Apostles, when they existed in their previous state, chosen to be blessed 'with all spiritual blessings in heavenly places in Christ?' "[19]

No doubt, the spirit children of Heavenly Father dwelt in his presence, saw him, and conversed with him, but that does not negate the need for them to exercise "exceedingly great faith" and to do good works, nor does it diminish the role of agency in the premortal realm. Even though children of earthly parents live in their parents' presence and earthly home, they still have agency to choose to disobey their parents' teachings, to be less than diligent in service and in family or church responsibilities, or to be persuaded by peers to do things that are not in harmony with the teachings of the gospel. It seems logical to assume that in some respects the spirit children of Heavenly Father exercised their agency in a manner similar to earthly children. To say that a spirit who dwells in the Father's presence could not or did not need to exercise faith in God denies what Alma wrote speaking of those priests who were chosen premortally because of their "exceedingly great faith." To assume that there was no sin in God's presence among the millions of his spirit children would be to minimize the indispensable roles of agency, opposition, and the knowledge of good and evil in the premortal world.

The scriptures and statements of the prophets indicate that there is, indeed, much similarity between the conditions of and expectations for mankind premortally and on earth. That gospel principles were taught and practiced in both places also implies that the atonement of Jesus Christ was in full effect in premortal world. Orson Pratt, speaking of sin in the premortal world, wrote that "among the two-thirds who remained, it is highly probable that there were many who were not valiant . . . , but whose sins were of such a nature that they could be forgiven through faith in the future sufferings of the Only Begotten of the Father, and through their sincere repentance and reformation. We see no impropriety in Jesus offering himself as an acceptable offering and sacrifice before the Father to atone for the sins of His brethren, committed, not only in the second, but also in the first estate."[20] This stimulating thought takes on additional significance when pondered in light of Alma's description of Christ's atonement as "an infinite and eternal sacrifice" (Alma 34:10).

The Lord may also have been referring to the premortal effects of the Atonement in modern revelation to the

Prophet Joseph: "Every spirit of man was innocent in the beginning; and God having redeemed man from the fall, men became again, in their infant state, innocent before God" (D&C 93:38). The key word is *again*. This seems to indicate that men had lost innocence in the premortal world through sin and disobedience, but were once again, through the great plan of redemption, made innocent before God upon entering mortality "in their infant state."

Finally, recognizing the role of agency and its contingent principles is paramount to obtaining a fuller understanding of the significance of man's premortal existence. This principle of premortal agency permeates virtually every aspect of the doctrine of premortal existence. Without it, it would be virtually impossible to understand the impact that a premortal existence had on the mortal sojourn of each child of God.

A House of Glory, a House of Beauty

While nothing has been revealed specifically concerning the appearance of the premortal world, there are some interesting statements from latter-day prophets that shed light on the subject. To the heavenly parents, it was a celestial kingdom. As discussed previously, the premortal estate served as a pattern or type in many ways for this temporal existence as well as for the postmortal spirit world. It is interesting to then "look back" at that premortal home through descriptions of those postmortal realms that are patterned after the first estate.

The Prophet Joseph Smith saw in vision the celestial kingdom and described its beauty and splendor. "The heavens were opened upon us, and I beheld the celestial kingdom of God, and the glory thereof. . . . I saw the transcendent beauty of the gate through which the heirs of that kingdom will enter, which was like unto circling flames of fire; Also the blazing throne of God, whereon was seated the Father and the Son. I saw the beautiful streets of that kingdom, which had the appearance of being paved with gold." (D&C 137:1–4.)

During a tour of the Church in the South Pacific in 1921, President David O. McKay, then a member of the Quorum of the Twelve, had a remarkable vision of the celestial kingdom. His description provides a glimpse of how the premortal heavenly home probably appeared.

> I . . . beheld in vision something infinitely sublime. In the distance I beheld a beautiful white city. Though far away, yet I seemed to realize that trees with luscious fruit, shrubbery with gorgeously tinted leaves, and flowers in perfect bloom abounded everywhere. The clear sky above seemed to reflect these beautiful shades of color. I then saw a great concourse of people approaching the city. Each one wore a white flowing robe, and a white headdress. Instantly my attention seemed centered upon their Leader, and though I could see only the profile of his features and his body, I recognized him at once as my Savior! The tint and radiance of his countenance were glorious to behold? There was a peace about him which seemed sublime—it was divine![21]

President Brigham Young spoke *specifically* of the premortal world when he declared that the spirit children of God were indeed "acquainted with every nook and corner, with the palaces, walks, and gardens" of that realm.[22] President Jedediah M. Grant saw in vision the beauty and grandeur of the postmortal spirit world. His descriptions reflect those conditions spoken of with regard to both the premortal and postmortal Celestial Kingdom. We can only wonder how close his description would apply to the first estate. "He spoke of the buildings he saw there," said Heber C. Kimball, "remarking that the Lord gave Solomon wisdom and poured gold and silver into his hands that he might display his skill and ability, and said that the temple erected by Solomon was much inferior to the most ordinary buildings he saw in the spirit world." Describing the gardens there, President Grant told Heber C. Kimball, "I have seen good gardens on this earth, but I never saw any to compare with those that were there. I saw flowers of numerous kinds, and some with from fifty to a hundred different colored flowers growing upon one stalk." Heber C. Kimball then concluded, "We have many kinds of flowers on the earth, and I suppose those very articles came from heaven, or they would not be here."[23]

Each of these prophetic descriptions portrays cities with magnificent buildings and gardens with spectacular foliage of many colors. There are descriptions of peace and glory in this heavenly home. As with President David O. McKay's description of the Savior, no doubt the appearance of the heavenly parents to their spirit children was equally sublime and glorious to behold. Seeing them in their celestial surroundings clothed with resurrected bodies of glory provided a visual reminder, no doubt, of the ultimate objective of the plan of redemption. While the actual physical description of the premortal heavenly home may not hold the same theological significance as the existence of such principles as agency or priesthood, the glory and beauty of the first estate must have served as a profound reminder of the eternal reward for those who would faithfully keep their second estate. Living in a heavenly house of beauty and glory may have created in us an innate spiritual "homesickness" and a desire to return to that celestial habitat.

Summary

Myriad unanswered questions remain concerning specific conditions in and the appearance of the premortal home. The Father has purposely withheld from his children a complete view of the premortal world, but he has given enough enlightenment to understand certain basic conditions. From the revealed words of prophets we begin to gain a clearer view of the first estate as a house of order and organization.

This order in God's house is a type for his kingdom on earth; and that same order facilitates the important work that is conducted in the spirit world. It is clear that the guiding power and directing influence in that house of order was, as it is on earth, the priesthood of God.

God's house is a house of agency. Agency prevails as an eternal principle that must exist in order for God's children to become exalted like himself. Understanding that agency existed premortally clarifies many other aspects of the premortal world such as the varying levels of progression and the impact of choices made in the premortal world on our mortal existence.

God's house is a house of glory and beauty. No glory or beauty can compare with that found in the presence of the exalted Father. No man can remember the exact scenes of the premortal home. Yet each man, if he will heed it, carries with him a subtle, yet innate, spiritual longing to return to those environs of splendor and glory and to once again experience the peace and sublimity of beholding the face of God.

Notes

1. Brigham Young, *Journal History*, February 23, 1847, as cited in Hyrum L. Andrus, *Doctrinal Commentary on the Pearl of Great Price* (Salt Lake City: Deseret Book Co., 1967), p. 122.

2. Heber C. Kimball, funeral address for Jedediah M. Grant, December 4, 1856; as quoted in *Doctrines from the Prophets*, compiled by Alma P. Burton, (Salt Lake City: Bookcraft, 1970), p. 423.

3. Joseph Fielding Smith, *The Way to Perfection* (Salt Lake City: Deseret Book Co., 1972), pp. 50–51.

4. Joseph Smith, *Teachings of the Prophet Joseph Smith*, (Salt Lake City: Deseret Book Co., 1972), pp. 166–167.

5. Wilford Woodruff, in *Journal of Discourses*, 21:318.

6. Joseph Fielding Smith, *Doctrines of Salvation* (Salt Lake City: Bookcraft, 1954), 3:81.

7. Brigham Young, in *Journal of Discourses*, 2:139.

8. John Taylor, *Millennial Star*, 9:321.

9. Stephen L Richards, as quoted by Ezra Taft Benson, in Conference Report, April 1979, p. 121.

10. Joseph Smith, *Teachings of the Prophet Joseph Smith*, p. 181.

11. Joseph F. Smith, in *Journal of Discourses*, 25:57.

12. The First Presidency (Joseph F. Smith, John R. Winder, Anthon H. Lund), "The Origin of Man," *Improvement Era*, November 1909, pp. 75–81.

13. Bruce R. McConkie, *Mormon Doctrine*, 2nd edition (Salt Lake City: Bookcraft, 1966), p. 26.

14. Joseph Smith, *Teachings of the Prophet Joseph Smith*, (Salt Lake City: Deseret Book Co., 1972), pp. 308, 324–325.

15. Brigham Young, in *Journal of Discourses*, 8:28.

16. Brigham Young, in *Journal of Discourses*, 4:268.

17. Joseph Fielding Smith, *Doctrines of Salvation*, 1:58–59.

18. Several scriptural passages state that "no unclean thing can dwell in God's presence" (see 1 Nephi 15:34; Alma 7:21; 11:37; 40:26; Helaman 8:25; 3 Nephi 27:19), but none of these passages have authoritatively been interpreted to have application to the premortal world. A careful examination of the context of these passages shows their specific reference to the *postmortal* judgment, resurrection, and salvation of God's children. In other words, no unclean or unsanctified person can be "saved" or exalted in God's kingdom, the celestial kingdom. D&C 76:51–52, 62 and D&C 84:14–21 clearly teach that dwelling in God's presence refers to postmortal exaltation.

19. Orson Pratt, *The Seer*, vol. 1, no. 4, p. 55.

20. Orson Pratt, *The Seer*, vol. 1, no. 4, p. 54.

21. David O. McKay, *Cherished Experiences from the Writings of President David O. McKay*, compiled by Clare Middlemiss (Salt Lake City: Deseret Book Co., 1976), p. 109.

22. Brigham Young, in *Journal of Discourses*, 4:268.

23. Heber C. Kimball, funeral address for Jedediah M. Grant, as quoted in *Doctrines from the Prophets*, comp. Alma P. Burton, pp. 423–424.

6

The War
in Heaven

Both ancient and modern revelation bear record of a profound event wherein all of the previously described conditions of agency, opposition, sin, repentance, and individual accountability were brought to bear. This event has become known as the War in Heaven. The ancient prophet Isaiah poetically described his vision of Lucifer's premortal rebellion. "How art thou fallen from heaven, O Lucifer, son of the morning! how art thou cut down to the ground, which didst weaken the nations! For thou hast said in thine heart, I will ascend into heaven, I will exalt my throne above the stars of God: I will sit also upon the mount of the congregation, in the sides of the north: I will ascend above the heights of the clouds; I will be like the most High. Yet thou shalt be brought down to hell, to the sides of the pit." (Isaiah 14:12–15.)

John the Revelator, using symbolic language, also referred to this premortal rebellion of Lucifer and the tragic consequences of the War in Heaven when he wrote that "there fell a great star from heaven, burning as it were a lamp, and it fell upon the third part of the rivers, and upon the fountains of waters; and the name of the star is called Wormwood: and the third part of the waters became wormwood; and many men died of the waters, because they were made bitter" (Revelation 8:10–11).

The significance of these scriptural passages is largely hidden from the world because it lacks the knowledge of the premortal life found in modern revelation. Although the War in Heaven is alluded to in both the Old and New Testaments, it is through the clarity of the modern records that we finally achieve an understanding of this event.

When Abraham saw in vision the premortal spirits, he noted that many were "noble and great ones" who were chosen to be rulers on earth. He saw the plan of salvation presented to the spirits and witnessed the Father's call for a savior to implement that plan on earth. Abraham's description of that event and subsequent events, though sketchy, enlightens us a little more concerning the War in Heaven. "And the Lord said: Whom shall I send? And one answered like unto the Son of Man: Here am I, send me. And another answered and said: Here am I, send me. And the Lord said: I will send the first. And the second was angry, and kept not his first estate; and, at that day, many followed after him." (Abraham 3:27–28.)

Abraham begins to identify the great issues of the War in Heaven that are vaguely alluded to in both the Old and New Testaments. But even the inspired account of Abraham, which was received by the Prophet Joseph, did not fully identify the issues nor the participants in this important premortal event. Joseph Smith brought forth another account which provides a few more important details. It came in the form of a revelation received by Moses after his personal encounter with Satan. Coupled with Abraham's vision, this revelation offers a greater understanding of the issues and events.

And I, the Lord God, spake unto Moses, saying: That Satan, whom thou hast commanded in the name of mine Only Begotten, is the same which was from the beginning, and he came before me, saying—Behold, here am I, send me, I will be thy son, and I will redeem all mankind, that one soul shall not be lost, and surely I will do it; wherefore give me thine honor.

But, behold, my Beloved Son, which was my Beloved and Chosen from the beginning, said unto me—Father, thy will be done, and the glory be thine forever.

Wherefore, because that Satan rebelled against me, and sought to destroy the agency of man, which I, the Lord God, had given him, and also, that I should give unto him mine own power; by the power of mine Only Begotten, I caused that he should be cast down;

And he became Satan, yea, even the devil, the father of all lies, to deceive and to blind men, and to lead them captive at his will, even as many as would not hearken unto my voice. (Moses 4:1–4.)

The Prophet Joseph also saw this great event in vision. The following record of what he saw serves as a preface to his vision of the three degrees of glory recorded in Doctrine and Covenants section 76.

And now, after the many testimonies which have been given of him, this is the testimony, last of all, which we give of him: That he lives!

For we saw him, even on the right hand of God; and we heard the voice bearing record that he is the Only Begotten of the Father—

That by him, and through him, and of him, the worlds are and were created, and the inhabitants thereof are begotten sons and daughters unto God.

And this we saw also, and bear record, that an angel of God who was in authority in the presence of God, who rebelled against the Only Begotten Son whom the Father loved and who was in the bosom of the Father, was thrust down from the presence of God and the Son,

And was called Perdition, for the heavens wept over him —he was Lucifer, a son of the morning.

And we beheld, and lo, he is fallen! is fallen, even a son of the morning! (D&C 76:22–27; see also D&C 29:36–38.)

These twelve verses from modern scripture, along with a few other isolated references, contribute a great deal to our grasp of the issues, actions, and characters associated with the War in Heaven. These few verses alone, however insightful and informative they may be, are still incomplete in giving us as meaningful and useful an understanding of the significance of that event as we might have. It is necessary to couple these passages from holy writ with the inspired statements of latter-day prophets. Moreover, we can examine carefully still other scattered scriptural references and ponder their implications to the premortal war in heaven, and consider the impact of that cataclysmic event on all of the children of God.

The Father's Plan

As discussed in a previous chapter, one of the conditions that prevailed in the premortal realm was that of instruction in the laws, principles, and ordinances of the plan of salvation. Some have attempted to promote the idea, by songs, scripts, and sermons, that two opposing plans were presented in the Grand Council for the Father's consideration and for the vote of acceptance by his children. Such an idea is contrary to the revealed word of God found in both the standard works and the writings of the prophets. There was only one plan presented and that plan was the Father's. Each spirit child had heard that plan taught and expounded in clarity and power. The Prophet Joseph affirmed that it was the Father who instituted and presented the plan. "God himself, finding he was in the midst of spirits and glory, because he was more intelligent, saw proper to institute laws whereby the rest could have a privilege to advance like himself."[1]

Addressing himself to the often-stated view in the Church that there were two plans presented at the Grand Council in Heaven, Elder Bruce R. McConkie wrote:

> Who created and presented the plan of salvation as it was adopted in the pre-existent councils in heaven? Did Christ offer one plan which would allow men their agency, and Lucifer sponsor another founded on compulsion?
>
> Although we sometimes hear it said that there were two plans—Christ's plan of freedom and agency, and Lucifer's of slavery and compulsion—such teaching does not conform to the revealed word. Christ did not present a plan of redemption and salvation nor did Lucifer. There were not two plans up for consideration; there was only one; and that was the plan of the Father: originated, developed, presented, and put in force by him. . . .
>
> The chief cornerstone of the whole plan was to be the atoning sacrifice of a Redeemer, one of the Father's spirit sons who was to be born into the world as his literal Son in the flesh. By this means was to be effected a resurrection, a reunion of body and spirit in immortality, the two never again to be separated.[2]

Thus, the plan that was presented in this Grand Council was the Father's plan—instituted to "bring to pass the immortality and eternal life of man" (Moses 1:39). It was not a question of *which* plan the Father would accept to implement for his children on earth, but rather a question of *whom* he could send, as Savior and Redeemer of the world, to implement that plan. Even then, there was really no question.

Whom Shall I Send?

When the Father asked, "Whom shall I send?" (Abraham 3:27), was he truly asking for volunteers to explain their personal qualifications and to petition for the right to be the Savior? Or was the question merely rhetorical, with an already determined answer? Were the spirit children of God really unsure about who would be the Savior under the Father's plan or was it already well known? A careful examination of the scriptural account and a study of the qualifications and motives of both Jesus and Lucifer suggest the answer.

Moses records that Jesus was the Father's "Beloved and Chosen from the beginning" (Moses 4:2). Other scriptural passages likewise depict Jesus Christ as the chosen and foreordained Savior of the world. The brother of Jared heard the premortal Christ declare: "Behold, I am he who was prepared from the foundation of the world to redeem my people. Behold, I am Jesus Christ." (Ether 3:14.) Peter also referred to Christ as He "who verily was foreordained before the foundation of the world" (1 Peter 1:20). These passages seem to confirm that Jesus was the Chosen of the Father not merely because of his affirmative response to the Father's query "Whom shall I send?" but rather because of who he was for the eons of time prior to that Grand Council.

Jesus Christ, the Firstborn of the Father in the Spirit

Numerous references in both the Old and New Testaments refer to the Messiah as being the "firstborn." In a messianic psalm, God is heard to speak of his Son by saying, "Also I will make him my firstborn" (Psalm 89:27). The Apostle Paul also speaks of Christ as "the firstborn of every creature" (Colossians 1:15) and "the firstborn among many brethren" (Romans 8:29). To the Hebrew Saints, Paul writes that the Father has described his Only Begotten as "the firstbegotten" (Hebrews 1:6).

The Hebrew word that is translated as "firstborn" is *bekor*, signifying "preeminent one" or "the attribute or quality of preeminence."

Undoubtedly, Jesus was selected to be the Savior under the Father's plan because he was spiritually preeminent, but the Savior's premortal preeminence takes on additional meaning through modern revelation. To the Prophet Joseph, Jesus declared: "And now, verily I say unto you, I was in the beginning with the Father, and am the Firstborn" (D&C 93:21). The literal nature of this statement has been affirmed by prophets in this dispensation. Elder Orson Pratt declared:

> Have you not read, in the New Testament, that Jesus Christ was the first-born of every creature? From this reading it would seem that he was the oldest of the whole human family, that is, so far as his birth in the spirit world is concerned. . . . Have you not also read in the New Testament that he is called our elder brother? Does this refer to the birth of the body of flesh and bones? By no means, for there were hundreds of millions who were born upon our earth before the body of flesh and bones was born whom we call Jesus. How is it, then, that he is our elder brother? We must go back to the previous birth, before the foundation of this earth; we have to go back to past ages, to the period when he was begotten of the Father among the great family of spirits.[3]

On two separate occasions the First Presidency of the Church confirmed that Jesus was indeed the firstborn of the spirit family of God. In 1909, President Joseph F. Smith, in "The Origin of Man," a statement by the First Presidency, declared that "the Father of Jesus is our Father also. Jesus Himself taught this truth, when He instructed His disciples how to pray: 'Our Father which art in heaven,' etc. Jesus, however, is the *firstborn among all the sons of God—the firstbegotten in the spirit*, and the only begotten in the flesh. He is our elder brother, and we, like Him, are in the image of God."[4]

And in 1916 a statement from the First Presidency and the Council of the Twelve appeared in the *Improvement Era*: "Among the spirit children of Elohim the firstborn was and is Jehovah or Jesus Christ to whom all others are juniors."[5]

Jesus, then, as the firstborn of all of the spirit children of God, was the Chosen of the Father, not only because of his preeminence among the spirits but also by virtue of his birthright as the firstborn. Elder Bruce R. McConkie wrote of the Savior: "Our Blessed Lord is the firstborn spirit child of the Father of spirits; all others are junior to him. His is the eternal birthright and the everlasting right of presidency."[6]

While we do not fully know to what extent this primogeniture operated in the premortal world, it appears that Jesus was the Chosen of the Father even prior to the Father asking, "Whom shall I send?" It was his right to be chosen as the Savior. Yet, as illustrated many times in the Old Testament, there is more to birthright responsibilities and blessings than just birth order. In the case of the great Jehovah, he received the birthright responsibility of redemption not only because of his status as firstborn of the spirits but also, as suggested by the Hebrew word *bekor*, because of his spiritual preeminence among the children of God.

Jesus Christ, "Like unto God"

In Abraham's vision of the premortal spirit hosts of heaven, when he saw "many of the noble and great ones" (Abraham 3:22), Jehovah stood foremost among them all. Of him Abraham records, "There stood one among them that was like unto God" (Abraham 3:24). Jesus was so outstanding among the spirits that Abraham characterizes him as "like unto God." This premortal preeminence was also alluded to in the writings of John the Beloved when he wrote that Christ, or the Word, was with God in the beginning, "and the Word [Christ] was God" (John 1:1). Of this godlike stature of Christ, Elder Bruce R. McConkie asked:

> Like unto God—how and in what way? Like him in length of days or the possession of progeny or the exalted nature of his tangible body? No, for the Son of the Father had yet to pass through a mortal probation, to overcome the world, to attain a resurrection, and to come back to his Father with his own glorious and tangible body. But like

him in intelligence, in knowledge and understanding, in the possession of truth, in conformity to divine law, and therefore in power. Like him in plan and purpose, in desires for righteousness, in a willingness to serve his brethren, in all things that lead to that fulness of the glory of the Father which none can receive until they live in the eternal family unit as he does. . . . Like him as a Creator of worlds and planets innumerable.[7]

Through eons of premortal time, Jehovah exercised his agency in such ways as to bring about godlike obedience and faithfulness. His diligence and devotion resulted in godlike intelligence and wisdom. His premortal life radiated purity and perfection, submission and sinlessness. He was first among the spirit children of God in service and sacrifice. His spiritual preeminence encompassed not only characteristics of righteousness and obedience, but also the qualities of love and compassion. Both mortally and premortally, Jesus did "not anything save it be for the benefit of the world; for he loveth the world, even that he layeth down his own life that he may draw all men unto him" (2 Nephi 26:24). Jesus was the Chosen One not only because he was the firstborn spirit child of God and like unto God in righteousness and obedience but also because of his preeminent "loving kindness and his long-suffering towards the children of men" (1 Nephi 19:9).

In light of the premortal stature of Christ, it appears more likely that the Father's question "Whom shall I send?" was an invitation for Jesus to publicly and voluntarily accept the calling and appointment that was his by birthright as the Firstborn, the Preeminent One. It was a call for our commitment and common consent rather than a request for resumes. The call was issued, "Whom shall I send?" All eyes fell expectantly upon one spirit—the Firstborn, the one that was "like unto God." Not only did the Father, in his omniscience, know who the Chosen was to be, but each spirit man and woman saw Jesus as the foreordained Redeemer—

"prepared from the foundation of the world." He was the best and most qualified of all the spirits; in fact, no other came close. He was there as he is now, as Elder Neal A. Maxwell characterized, "utterly incomparable in what He *is*, what He *knows*, what He has *accomplished*, and what He has *experienced. . . .* In *intelligence* and *performance*, He far surpasses the individual and the composite *capacities* and *achievements* of all who have lived, live now, and will yet live! . . . He rejoices in our genuine goodness and achievement, but any assessment of where we stand in relation to Him tells us that we do not stand at all! We kneel!"[8]

Man's memory of this monumental moment is veiled by a divinely imposed forgetfulness. Even the scriptures cannot completely convey its spiritual significance and eternal consequence. Elder Orson F. Whitney attempted to visualize this event in his epic poem *Elias*. He imagined not only the events but also the emotions associated with the Savior's loving and voluntary submission to the Father's will.

A stature mingling strength with grace
Of meek though Godlike mien,
The love-revealing countenance
Lustrous as lightning sheen.
Whiter his hair than ocean spray,
Or frost of alpine hill.
He spake;—attention grew more grave,
The stillness e'en more still.

"Father!"—the voice like music fell,
Clear as the murmuring flow
Of mountain streamlet trickling down
From heights of virgin snow.
"Father," it said, "since one must die,
Thy children to redeem,
Whilst earth, as yet unformed and void,
With pulsing life shall teem;

And thou, great Michael, foremost fall,
That mortal man may be,

And chosen Saviour yet must send,
Lo, here am I—send me!
I ask, I seek no recompense,
Save that which then were mine;
Mine be the willing sacrifice,
The endless glory, Thine!⁹

"Here am I, send me," was Jehovah's response. This was no egotistical request for greater power or responsibility, but rather a humble acceptance of the Father's will—though that required a most awesome and agonizing obligation. His response, at the time of his premortal acceptance of his divine calling and foreordained mission, was the same as it was much later in its fulfillment in Gethsemane: "O my Father, if it be possible, let this cup pass from me: nevertheless not as I will, but as thou wilt" (Matthew 26:39). With Jehovah's acceptance, the heavenly home was filled with sounds of jubilation; for as Job records, "The morning stars sang together, and all the sons of God shouted for joy" (Job 38:7).

Lucifer's Rebellion

Not all were filled with joy and rejoicing, for there was one consumed with jealousy and resentment. The shouts of joy were soon shattered by the resonance of rebellion. The scriptures record that "an angel of God who was in authority in the presence of God . . . rebelled against the Only Begotten Son whom the Father loved and who was in the bosom of the Father. . . . He was Lucifer, a son of the morning." (D&C 76:25– 26.) From this brief scriptural statement, a picture of Lucifer as the instigator of rebellion and as a major combatant begins to emerge. In order to understand more fully *what* he proposed, *why* he proposed it, and *how* he led away so many, it is important to see *who* Lucifer was and is.

From his vision recorded in Doctrine and Covenants section 76 the Prophet Joseph Smith learned two major characteristics of Lucifer. First, Lucifer was "an angel of God who was in authority." No doubt he possessed great talents and abilities, for the name Lucifer literally means "the Shining One" and "lightbringer" (see Bible Dictionary, LDS edition of the Bible, p. 726). This certainly connotes that he was a leader among the spirits, possessing powers of persuasion. He had obtained great knowledge and no doubt was articulate and impressive. How much authority and power had been entrusted to him, the records do not say; but he was "in authority" and thus respected by others. President George Q. Cannon said, "This angel was a mighty personage, without doubt. The record that is given to us concerning him clearly shows that he occupied a very high position; that he was thought a great deal of, and that he was mighty in his sphere."[10]

Through his exercise of agency and his adherence to the laws and principles of the premortal world, Lucifer also "gained for himself great executive and administrative ability" and possessed a "compelling personality."[11]

The second thing the Prophet Joseph learned from the vision recorded in Doctrine and Covenants section 76 was that Lucifer was called "a son of the morning." While this term is usually associated with Lucifer's prominence and authority, there may also be another meaning, though of lesser significance. In this secondary sense, "son of the morning" has been interpreted to have reference to his place in the birth order of the spirit offspring of God. He was a "son of the morning," meaning one of the early spirit children. Elder Bruce R. McConkie has defined the term "son of the morning" thus: "This name-title of Satan indicates he was one of the early born spirit children of the Father. Always used in association with the name *Lucifer, son of the morning* also apparently signifies *son of light* or *son of prominence,* meaning that Satan held a position of power and authority in preexistence. (D&C 76:25–27; Isaiah 14:12–20.)"[12] Although he was indeed "a son of the morning," the idea that Lucifer was second only to Jehovah in authority and spiritual age is not substantiated in the revelations. He was, however, one of the older spirit children and thus, by virtue of his authoritative prominence and spiritual age, he commanded an element of respect from his younger spirit siblings.

Despite Lucifer's prominence and authority in the premortal realms, he would not sustain the Father's plan. With Jesus' acceptance of his apparently preordained calling as "the Lamb . . . slain from the foundation of the world" (Moses 7:47), Lucifer rebelled. In lieu of consent, there was contention. Modern revelation specifically shows the direction in which Lucifer's anger was aimed. "And this we saw also, and bear record, that an angel of God who was in authority in the presence of God . . . *rebelled against the Only Begotten Son* whom the Father loved and who was in the bosom of the Father" (D&C 76:25; italics added).

Why would Lucifer, the "Shining One" who had been taught the Father's plan of salvation and who had risen in authority by virtue of his apparent faithfulness, now rebel against Him whom the Father had chosen and "prepared from the foundation of the world" (Ether 3:14)? Elder Mark E. Petersen indicates that despite his strengths, Lucifer's weaknesses brought about his rebellion and resentment. Foremost among his character defects were his pride, selfishness, and jealousy. Elder Petersen suggests that Lucifer "coveted honor, prestige and glory; he wanted the adulation and praise of others; he sought to be lifted up above the rest. What an egotist! Lucifer hated his elder brother, Jehovah. . . . Blinded by jealousy . . . he sought to thwart everything that Jehovah stood for, everything Jehovah did."[13]

Had Lucifer deceived the Father all along? Had he obtained his authority in the presence of God by fraud? Had his faithfulness and obedience been feigned for so long? While there are no authoritative answers to such questions, it seems unlikely that any spirit obtained authority or rose in prominence by deception. The omniscient Father was not fooled. It is more likely that Lucifer had indeed been faithful and thus had been rewarded with greater authority and responsibility. Perhaps latent in Lucifer, as in some during mortality, were the tendencies to "aspire to the honors of men," to "gratify . . . pride, . . . vain ambition, or to exercise control or dominion or compulsion upon the souls of the children of men" (D&C 121:35, 37). It may be that Lucifer, in the premortal pride of his own prominence, experienced the lesson the Lord later taught: "We have learned by sad experience that it is the nature and disposition of almost all men, as soon as they get a little authority, as they suppose, they will immediately begin to exercise unrighteous dominion" (D&C 121:39). With this conceited sense of self-importance, Lucifer deceived himself and thus became "a liar from the beginning" (D&C 93:25).

It was in this spirit of self-deception, pride, and arrogant ambition that Lucifer boldly declared to the Father, "Behold, here am I, send me, I will be thy son, and *I will redeem all mankind, that one soul shall not be lost,* and surely I will do it; wherefore *give me thine honor*" (Moses 4:1; italics added). For Lucifer to even suggest a change in the plan was the ultimate arrogance. This is especially evident in the fact that Lucifer did not advocate that he be the Savior *under the Father's plan,* as Jesus had been chosen so to do. Neither did he ask to be considered to be the redeemer based solely on his own spiritual qualifications and worthiness. Since there was no comparison between him and Jehovah, he offered an alternative that would discredit the Father's plan and repudiate the divine appointment of Christ. So self-deluded was Lucifer that his counterproposal contained two egotistical elements — "Give me thine honor" and "I will redeem all mankind, that one soul shall not be lost." Elder Orson F. Whitney sought to depict this diabolical moment also in another segment of the previously quoted poem *Elias.*

> Silence once more. Then sudden rose
> Aloft a towering form,
> Proudly erect as lowering peak

'Lumed by the gathering storm!
A presence bright and beautiful,
With eye of flashing fire,
A lip whose haughty curl bespoke
A sense of inward ire.

"Give me to go!" thus boldly cried,
With scarce concealed disdain;
"And hence shall none, from heaven to earth,
That shall not rise again.
My saving plan exception scorns;
Man's agency unknown;
As recompense, I claim the right
to sit on yonder throne!"

"Give Me Thine Honor"

Lucifer's demand that he be given all of the Father's power, honor, and glory was evidence of his consummate conceit. The general principle of honor and glory, however, was not the issue of Lucifer's demand. Even Jesus recognized that synonymous with eternal life are the blessings of power, glory, and honor. Praying in Gethsemane, Jesus petitioned the Father "Glorify thou me *with thine own self* with the glory which I had *with thee* before the world was" (John 17:5; italics added). To all of his children, including Jesus, the Father had promised as a blessing of exaltation "all that [the] Father hath" (D&C 84:38), which would include "thrones, kingdoms, principalities, and powers, dominions, all heights and depths . . . and glory in all things" (D&C 132:19). Of the faithful Saints, who through obedience and sanctification would obtain crowns of eternal life, the Lord said, "Then shall they be above all, because all things are subject unto them. Then shall they be gods, because they have all power." (D&C 132:20.) Lucifer, however, rejected this honor, glory, and power that could have been his through faithful adherence to the Father's plan. He desired something more— something defiantly devilish.

The prophet Isaiah accurately portrayed the real meaning of Lucifer's demand for God's honor when he lamented, "How art thou fallen from heaven, O Lucifer, son of the morning! how art thou cut down to the ground which didst weaken the nations! For thou hast said in thine heart, I will ascend into heaven, *I will exalt my throne above the stars of God:* I will sit also upon the mount of the congregation, in the sides of the north: I will ascend *above* the heights of the clouds; *I will be like the most High.*" (Isaiah 14:12–14; italics added.) The Lord himself confirmed this to Moses when he told him through revelation that Satan "rebelled against me" and sought "that I should give unto him mine own power" (Moses 4:3).

Lucifer rejected the glory and honor and power of eternal life *with the Father* and desired instead to exalt himself *above the Father.* He had seen the glory of the Father and the esteem in which the Father was held by his children, and Lucifer desired that adulation even if it meant the elimination of the Father. He desired to supplant the Father and the Father's plan with his own fiendish, egocentric designs. Of this, Elder Orson Pratt wrote Lucifer "considered that his plan was so good before the heavens, and so much superior to the plan that God had devised, said he, 'Surely I will do it; wherefore give me thine honor, which is the power of God.' That is, he sought to obtain the throne of the Almighty, and to carry out his own purposes in preference to yielding to the purposes and power of the Almighty."[14] Lucifer was seeking something that neither was nor ever could be his. Elder Orson F. Whitney affirmed that "this 'Son of the Morning' had become darkened to that degree that he demanded, in recompense for his proposed service, the honor and glory that belong only to the Highest."[15] President J. Reuben Clark suggested that Satan wanted Heavenly Father to "abdicate," "disappear," "get out of the picture," so that he could "take over all the spirits in the great council and save them all."[16]

Implicit in Lucifer's demand for God's glory and honor was his plan for exaltation without effort. "I will exalt my throne [myself] above the stars of God," he declared. His declaration of self-exaltation exposed anew his jealousy of and resentment of Jesus the Redeemer. He would exalt himself *without* the redemptive blood of the great Jehovah. In his deluded and grandiose scheme of self-exaltation, he vainly imagined that he could, without the Savior's sacrifice, "redeem all mankind, that one soul shall not be lost."

"I Will Redeem All Mankind"

The Prophet Joseph Smith clearly identified that the methodology of salvation was the major issue in the Grand Council. "The contention in heaven was—Jesus said there would be certain souls that would not be saved; and the devil said he could save them all, and laid his plans before the grand council, who gave their vote in favor of Jesus Christ. So the devil rose up in rebellion against God, and was cast down, with all who put up their heads for him."[17]

The scriptures record that when Lucifer offered to save all, he "sought to destroy the agency of man" (Moses 4:3). This destruction of God-given agency was to be the result, not the proposition itself. Lucifer purposely and deceptively withheld any mention of the negative side effects of his prescription for salvation. By virtue of the claim that he would save all, Lucifer was covertly seeking to destroy the agency of man. The logic of his plan, or lack of it, is exposed in this statement by Elder Bruce R. McConkie:

> [Under Lucifer's plan], none would be damned; damnation would not be a viable alternative to salvation; there would be no agency—no freedom of choice, no election to serve God or to flee from evil and turn to righteousness. But if there is no freedom of choice between damnation and salva-

tion, how can either exist? They are opposites; without one you cannot have the other. . . .

. . . To be like him [God] is to gain eternal life. To gain this greatest of all rewards, the seeker of salvation must be free to choose between the Lord and Lucifer, for without the damnation of the devil, there can be no salvation with the Savior.[18]

Motives: Why Lucifer Sought to Destroy Agency

It is important to emphasize that Lucifer did not offer himself to be the savior under the Father's plan. When he responded, "Here am I, send me," he was in essence saying, "He am I, send me. I will be the redeemer of the world, but not under the conditions of the Father's plan. I will redeem all, *but it must be on my terms* and I must receive all glory and honor."

To understand the motives behind this proposal, one must understand the expectations and requirements facing that future Redeemer. Jesus knowingly and willingly accepted the demands to which he would be subjected in his redemptive role. He understood that to fulfill that magnificent mission, justice would require that he suffer "the pains of all men, yea, the pains of every living creature" (2 Nephi 9:21). No doubt he foresaw the scourging and the taunts of ridicule inflicted by his persecutors. Undoubtedly, the chosen Savior and all spirits knew that the Redeemer must be "in all points tempted like as we are, yet without sin" (Hebrews 4:15).

In stark contrast to the courage and compassion shown in Christ's acceptance of his status as Savior, Lucifer's demand to be a savior on his own terms conveys his own cowardice and contempt for man. In his selfishness and cowardice, Lucifer sought to destroy agency because he understood that with agency and opposition there would inevitably be sin. If man because of agency committed sin, justice required a painful payment. Lucifer cowered at the prospects of such supreme suffering. For the demands of justice to be met, the sufferer must also be sinless. Despite his self-deception, Lucifer knew that he could not be sinless because he had not thus far been sinless. Jesus was willing to do all this because of his love for us. Lucifer, on the other hand, rejected the Father's plan not only because of his own cowardice but also because he lacked the love for his siblings that was so abundant in Jehovah. It seems Lucifer knew that if mankind had agency, he, Lucifer, could not be the redeemer, for he recoiled from the responsibilities of redemption. He was a coward, a liar, an egotist; and thus, through his cleverly worded plan, he "sought to destroy the agency of man." President David O. McKay identified the "impelling motives" that were hidden in the heart of Lucifer.

> Man's free agency is fundamental to progress. An attempt to rob him of his free agency caused contention even in heaven.
>
> In that rebellion Lucifer said in substance: By the law of force I will compel the human family to subscribe to the eternal plan, but give me thine honor and power. To deprive an intelligent being of his free agency is to commit the crime of the ages.
>
> Impelling motives of this arch-enemy to liberty were pride, ambition, a sense of superiority, a will to dominate his fellows, and to be exalted above them, and a determination to deprive human beings of their freedom to speak and to act as their reason and judgment would dictate.[19]

How Lucifer Proposed to Redeem All Men

Other statements of latter-day prophets also confirm that Lucifer's agency-destroying proposition would indeed have caused men to be acted upon rather than to act for themselves. Perhaps one element of this proposal was even more insidious than the implied compulsion of men. Both Elder

Orson Pratt and Elder B. H. Roberts have highlighted that important element. "An agency was given to all intelligent beings," wrote Elder Pratt, "and without a proper agency, intelligent beings could not receive glory and honor, and a reward and a fullness of happiness in the celestial kingdom. There must be an agency wherever intelligence exists, and without agency no intelligent beings could exist; and . . . Satan sought to destroy this . . . *and to redeem them all in their sins*."[20] Elder B. H. Roberts added:

> Under this plan, Intelligences were to have an earthlife in which there would be no losses; a world where there was nothing adventurous and dangerous, a "game" in which there are no real stakes; all that was "hazarded" would be given back. All must be saved; and *no price is to be paid in the work of salvation*. . . . There could be no seriousness attributed to life under such a plan, since there were to be no insuperable "noes" and "losses"; no genuine sacrifices anywhere; . . . Man was to have nothing to do in the achievement, all was to be done for him. He was to be passive, merely. Not a thing to act, but something to be acted upon. Such only could be the outcome of a world where all mankind would be saved, "that not one soul should be lost."[21]

To implement a plan where there would be guaranteed salvation, exaltation without effort, and a life without sacrifice or suffering was theologically impossible. Lucifer's plan flew in the face of eternal laws and could not have worked even if all of the spirit offspring of God had "voted" for it. Elder Bruce R. McConkie confirmed that despite his powers of persuasion, "Lucifer's proposal to amend the Father's plan could not be; it was philosophically impossible to accomplish. He could not save all mankind, because unless some were damned, there would be no salvation, for nothing can so much as exist unless it has an opposite. Agency and freedom of worship are just that basic and important in the eternal plan of salvation."[22]

Since Lucifer's proposal was illogical, unworkable, and contrary to the laws of heaven, one must consider some important questions. How could such a "philosophically impossible" plan cause so much contention and consternation in heaven? Abraham records that "many followed after him" (Abraham 3:28). One cannot help but wonder how so many could be led away. These spirit children had been carefully and systematically taught the principles of the plan. Amidst such teachings, which were accompanied by power and authority, how could so many of the spirits see Lucifer's hodgepodge of heresy as a viable alternative to the Father's plan? Perhaps even more important than his motives, Lucifer's methods provide the answer.

Methods: Why Lucifer's Plan Was So Alluring

The Book of Mormon sheds valuable light on the methodology of Lucifer. Contained in that ancient record are accounts of three separate "anti-Christs" who had been tutored in their cunning crafts by Lucifer, "the father of all lies." All three of these notorious characters from the Book of Mormon were like Lucifer in their desires to disrupt and destroy the Father's plan. Each, in his own unique way, was also rebelling against the Only Begotten. The doctrines and characteristics of two of these anti-Christs, Sherem and Nehor, show remarkable similarities to the premortal preaching and persuading of Lucifer. By examining the scriptural sketches of these characters, we can expose the often subtle yet cunning tactics of Lucifer. In addition, we can better understand Lucifer's premortal duplicity.

The prophet Jacob wrote that Sherem "began to preach among the people, and to declare unto them *that there should be no Christ. And he preached many things which were flattering unto the people*; and this he did that he might overthrow the doctrine of Christ." (Jacob 7:2; italics added.) Another striking resemblance to Lucifer emerges in Jacob's further description of Sherem. "And he was *learned*, that he had a *perfect knowledge of the language* of the people; wherefore, he could use *much flattery* and *much power of speech*, according to the power of the devil" (Jacob 7:4; italics added).

Nehor, another anti-Christ, "testified unto the people that *all mankind should be saved at the last day*, and that they need not fear nor tremble . . . for the Lord . . . had also redeemed all men; and, in the end, *all men should have eternal life*" (Alma 1:4; italics added). Mormon's character description of Nehor reflects many of the same traits that were evident in Lucifer. "And it came to pass that *he did teach these things so much that many did believe on his words*. . . . And he began to be *lifted up in the pride of his heart* . . . and even began to establish a church after the manner of his preaching." (Alma 1:5–6; italics added.) It is also interesting to note that Alma says that Nehor was attempting to force or compel the people, even "by the sword," to believe his doctrine.

Undoubtedly Lucifer far surpassed even Sherem and Nehor in this knowledge and eloquence and flattery. It seems likely that through his powers of persuasion he magnified the trials and pitfalls of mortality that would be inevitable under the Father's plan. He may have painted, through his "power of speech," such a scene of suffering that many spirits doubted and despaired—doubted they would be able to be valiant under such conditions of agency and opposition, and despaired that they would ever be able to return to the Father's presence. It seems unlikely that Lucifer advocated force or compulsion; but probably, after creating a scenario of fear and misery, he introduced a most interesting and enticing plan. His easy, effortless plan must have seemed a stark contrast to the frightful description he would have given of the Father's plan, and those who wanted a smooth and simplified path through life must have been attracted to it. Regarding the attraction and enticement of Lucifer's plan,

Robert J. Matthews, dean of Religious Education at Brigham Young University, has provided this valuable insight:

> When we talk about our relationship to the Savior and our redemption, we must begin with the premortal life. I think we often miss the real issue of the contention in the spirit world that eventually led to the War in Heaven. We talk about it as though Lucifer were going to force everybody to obey. Most people don't want to be forced. As I see it, the real issue is that Lucifer would *guarantee their salvation. He promised salvation without effort, without excellence, without hard work, without individual responsibility.* That's the lie that he promulgated in the pre-earth councils. That so-called shortcut to salvation captivated many gullible and lazy spirits. They wanted something for nothing. We have certain aspects of that in our life today where things are awkward, something for nothing—a free lunch, we sometimes call it—with certain kinds of subsidies which promise to guarantee the reward without the effort. On that basis Lucifer led away many spirits.[23]

It begins to make sense that many could be lured away when Lucifer's plan is portrayed not so much as one of force but as one of freedom from accountability. In contrast to the inevitable casualties under a plan of agency and opposition, Lucifer's guarantee of salvation without effort was indeed attractive and enticing. So powerful were Lucifer's arguments about the dangers of mortality that the spirits could perhaps graphically visualize the stressful scenes of mortality. It was under the conditions of stress and fear that Lucifer's methods were most effective. Rabbi Harold S. Kushner, the author of such best-selling books as *When Bad Things Happen to Good People* and *When All You've Ever Wanted Is Not Enough*, made this interesting observation which parallels the premortal situation:

> There is a part of us, especially in times of stress, that wants to be cuddled and taken care of, to be told, "There's nothing to worry about; I'll take care of everything for you." . . . There is a part of us that wants somebody else to step in

and do all the hard things that we are supposed to do, relieving us of responsibility. . . .

. . . Erich Fromm, after fleeing from Nazi Germany to the United States, tried to understand how a cultured, educated people like the Germans could have let a man like Hitler come to power. In his book *Escape from Freedom*, he suggests an answer. Sometimes, he says, the problems of life become so overwhelming that we despair of ever solving them. Should someone come along and say in a loud, confident voice, "Follow me without question, do everything I tell you to, and I will lead you out of this," many of us would find that a very tempting offer. When life becomes difficult, we want someone to say to us, "Don't worry your little head about it. Let me do it for you, and all I want in return is your gratitude and total obedience."[24]

However attractive and alluring Lucifer's plan was, it was nonetheless an assault on the Father's plan and a futile attempt to redeem all mankind. "If you undertake to save all," wrote Brigham Young, "you must save them in unrighteousness and corruption."[25] Lucifer's plan was at odds with all the laws of heaven. He sought, as President John Taylor said, to "introduce something that was contrary to the law of God and to the counsel of God." His great sin was not just in his plan, but, more important, in his "departure from God and his laws, and because [he] sought to pervert the counsel of God, and violate those principles which [God] had introduced for the salvation of the world which was to be."[26]

Lucifer and His Followers Are Cast Out of Heaven

The scriptures and the prophets are silent regarding the actual nature and length of this event called the War in Heaven. "In regard to the battle in heaven," said Brigham Young, ". . . how much of a battle it was I have forgotten. I cannot relate the principal circumstances, it is so long since it happened."[27] Although the Lord has not directly revealed the particulars regarding this event, there are important inferences that can be made from careful examination of significant scriptural passages.

John the Revelator described his vision of Lucifer's rebellion and his ultimate banishment from God's presence. Several key words and phrases in his description illuminate the manner of warfare that prevailed in the War in Heaven.

> And there was war in heaven: Michael and his angels fought against the dragon; and the dragon fought and his angels,
>
> And prevailed not; neither was their place found any more in heaven.
>
> And the great dragon was cast out, that old serpent, called the Devil, and Satan, which deceiveth the whole world: he was cast out into the earth, and his angels were cast out with him.
>
> And I heard a loud voice saying in heaven, Now is come salvation, and strength, and the kingdom of our God, and the power of his Christ: *for the accuser of our brethren is cast down, which accused them before our God day and night.*
>
> And they overcame him by the blood of the Lamb, and by the word of their testimony; and they loved not their lives unto the death. (Revelation 12:7–11; italics added.)

It is interesting that John refers to Lucifer as "the accuser of our brethren." The Greek word from which "accuser" was translated in the New Testament had a broader meaning in classical Greek, which could connote "a betrayer," "a denouncer," or one who "speaks evil of another." This insight certainly shows that Lucifer's rebellion may have begun merely with his proposal but ended with his total rebellion, his betrayal and denouncement of both the Father and His Beloved and Chosen Son.

Nothing could be further from the truth than to portray the banishment of Lucifer and "a third part of the hosts of heaven" (D&C 29:36) as the result of a simple vote for Lucifer's plan. It seems unthinkable that a merciful and loving

Father would banish a third of his spirit children to an everlasting punishment simply because they "voted wrong" and chose Lucifer's proposal. The War in Heaven involved much more than just voting for plans of salvation. It undoubtedly involved a war of words, a war for the hearts, minds, souls, and strength of all of God's children. It was the ultimate premortal test of each spirit's valiance, commitment, and love for the Father. Those who, with Lucifer, were cast out, were cast out because they had been, figuratively and literally, accusers of their brethren.

In the literal sense, it may have been that Lucifer and his followers "accused" Jehovah and the brethren before the Father, much like Korihor, the third anti-Christ mentioned in the Book of Mormon, denounced and accused the prophet Alma. Korihor accused Alma of oppressing the people and not allowing them to think for themselves. He said their religious beliefs were "the effect of a frenzied mind; and this derangement of your minds comes because of the traditions of your fathers, which lead you away into a belief of things which are not so" (Alma 30:16).

Almost like echoes from eternity past, one can logically hear Lucifer using the same types of arguments as he denounced Jehovah. He may have accused him of oppressing and misleading the spirit children of God so that he might have power over them. Perhaps, because of the perils inherent in the Father's plan, Satan could cleverly (though falsely) accuse Jehovah of indifference towards his brothers and sisters, since many would be lost. On the other hand, he would have upheld himself as compassionate and concerned by virtue of his liberal plan of non-salvation. Like Korihor in his assault on Alma, Satan would have twisted the truth, calling good evil and evil good. He was the prototype for those whom the Lord has unequivocally denounced in the scriptures: "Cursed are all those that shall lift up the heel against mine anointed, saith the Lord, and cry they have sinned when they have not sinned before me, saith the Lord, but have done that which was meet in mine eyes, and which I commanded them. But those who cry transgression do it because they are the servants of sin, and are the children of disobedience themselves. And [cursed are] those who swear falsely against my servants, that they might bring them into bondage and death." (D&C 121:16–18.) How perfectly this description fits both Korihor and Lucifer in their efforts to discredit and accuse God's "anointed." Furthermore, Lucifer and his ardent and zealous supporters, in their efforts to win the war for souls, accused, denounced, swore falsely against, and spoke evil of not only Jehovah but also the Father and all who supported the true plan of salvation.

In the figurative sense, Lucifer was the "accuser" in that he was, in verity, a betrayer. He not only betrayed the Father and Jehovah but also openly and defiantly betrayed and sought to undermine all those laws, principles, and teachings that he, himself, previously had known to be true. He became Perdition, and his followers, sons of perdition, in the same way that mortals can descend to such depths. The scriptures explain this descent, which applies to premortal souls much the same as to mortals. The Prophet Joseph learned that those who are cast out to "eternal punishment" in a place "where their worm dieth not, and the fire is not quenched" (D&C 76:44) are those who have "denied the Holy Spirit after having received it" and have also "denied the Only Begotten Son of the Father, having crucified him unto themselves and put him to an open shame" (D&C 76:35). They have, as the Prophet Joseph declared of those who suffer this fate, denied Jesus Christ after they have understood in clarity and surety the Father's plan. They have refused the plan of salvation with their "eyes open to the truth of it." They are determined to make "open war" against the plan of salvation.[28]

While we may not know fully what happened in this war, we can see that it was of such severity that many lost their hope for salvation as a result of their sins. Elder Orson Pratt made this illuminating statement on the nature and duration of the war, and also on the nature of the sins that resulted in the expulsion of Lucifer and a third part of the spirits.

> It is not likely that the final decision of the contending armies took place immediately. Many, no doubt, were unsettled in their views, unstable in their minds, and undecided as to which force to join: there may have been, for aught we know, many deserters from both armies: and there may have been a long period before the division line was so strictly drawn as to become unalterable. Laws, without doubt, were enacted, and penalties affixed, according to the nature of the offences or crimes: those who altogether turned from the Lord, and were determined to maintain the cause of Satan, and who proceeded to the *utmost extremities of wickedness*, placed themselves without the reach of redemption: therefore, such were prohibited from entering into a second probationary state, and had no privilege of receiving bodies of flesh and bones. . . .
>
> Among the two thirds who remained, it is highly probable that there were many who were not valiant in the war, but whose sins were of such a nature that they could be forgiven through faith in the future sufferings of the Only Begotten of the Father, and through their sincere repentance and reformation.[29]

Lucifer and his followers were not cast out of heaven merely because they had unwittingly proposed and supported an illogical plan, but through their open rebellion, their betrayal of the Father and Son, and because their sins were of the "utmost extremities of wickedness," the redemptive power of Christ's atonement could have no claim on them. As Elder Bruce R. McConkie has written:

> Because of their open rebellion against light and truth, because they defied God and his government, knowing perfectly what the will of the Father was, they were cast out of heaven onto this earth. Their punishment: eternal damnation. Progression ceased for them. No mortal bodies would ever house their spirit forms. For them there was to be no second estate, no probationary experiences, no resurrection,

no eternal life—nothing but darkness and defiance; nothing but wickedness and rebellion; nothing but hatred and evil to all eternity, because they came out in open rebellion and with a perfect knowledge of the course they then pursued and of the consequences that attended it; they fought against God. It is an awful thing to defy the Lord, to make open warfare against the Supreme Being.[30]

Lucifer lost the War in Heaven and "was thrust down from the presence of God and the Son, and was called Perdition, for the heavens wept over him" (D&C 76:25–26). Michael and his angels defeated Lucifer and one third of the hosts of heaven by the power of the Only Begotten Son in this premortal war, but the war for the hearts and souls of the other two thirds of God's children rages on.

The War in Heaven Continues on Earth

The Prophet Joseph, who saw the premortal rebellion of Lucifer, also saw and described the continuation of the conflict: "For we beheld Satan, that old serpent, even the devil, who rebelled against God, and sought to take the kingdom of our God and his Christ—Wherefore, he maketh war with the saints of God, and encompasseth them round about. And we saw a vision of the sufferings of those with whom he made war and overcame." (D&C 76:28–30.) The war that commenced in the premortal realm of God continues here on earth. The participants are the same. The methods and motives of Lucifer have not changed, for he continues to seek to destroy the agency of man. Since he desires desperately the "full possession, ownership" of all the spirits of men, and since he could not "get them by gift," he has followed us here to earth "trying to get us through the commission of sin. If we sin sufficiently we become his subjects."[31] While it may not always seem like a battleground, the invisible enemy is real and the efforts needed to defeat him here, as there, have not diminished. President Wilford Woodruff said of this continuing conflict:

[Lucifer] has great influence over the children of men; he labors continually to destroy the works of God in heaven, and he had to be cast out. He is here, mighty among the children of men. There is a vast number of fallen spirits, cast out with him, here on earth. They do not die and disappear; they have not bodies only as they enter the tabernacles of men. They have not organized bodies, and are not to be seen with the sight of the eye. But there are many evil spirits amongst us, and they labor to overthrow the church and kingdom of God. . . .

. . . Do you suppose these devils are around us without trying to do something? . . . I say . . . we have got a mighty warfare to wage with these spirits. We cannot escape it. What will they do to you? They will try to make us do anything and everything that is not right.[32]

The character and methodology of Lucifer in the premortal world can best be understood by observing his warring works as they continue on earth. Elder Mark E. Petersen has fittingly described the War in Heaven that now rages on earth as "the longest war." Satan's premortal motives and methods are now exemplified and amplified with satanic fervor by those spirits who followed him to his newest battleground—earth.

Cast out of heaven, Lucifer and his devilish host turned to the next step in their nefarious warfare—enticement!

They had wanted to become mortals and have physical bodies like ours, but were defeated by their own rebellion. However, they knew that mortals would be subject to sin and would have weaknesses, and that many of them would surrender to enticement.

So Lucifer's army turned to temptation as their most effective weapon. They would induce these mortals to sin and by this means endeavor to defeat the purposes of Jehovah. . . .

Now he sought to prevent all of us from becoming like our Father in heaven as we use the right means, the way provided by Jehovah. Seeing that the gospel plan truly can make mortals perfect like God only added to the frustration of Lucifer. . . .

He knows what exaltation means, for he saw it as he lived in the presence of God. . . .

He knows that "all that my Father hath" shall be given to His faithful children (D&C 84:38), and he knows that such is now forever beyond his reach. So once again in him there arises deeper frustration, sharper resentment, and more vicious anger.

Jealousy against the Savior and all of his Saints increases in his evil heart. He uses every tool of enticement and temptation to accomplish his wicked ends. Inasmuch as he himself now can never be exalted, he tries to prevent all others from achieving that goal.

What does he care about us, except to destroy us? We are his targets, we are his prey. With lies and intrigue he would persuade us that happiness may be found in sin, that gain may be had through fraud, deception, licentiousness, and even murder.

By his glamor he would blind us to the end result of sin. He would make it seem attractive, even though he knows that its wage is death.

He lures us by the lust of the flesh. He resents "the flesh" because he knows that he himself can never have it. . . .

He therefore tempts us according to the flesh with sex, money, greed, worldly prestige, ease, comfort, and a loose and carefree life.

With it he introduces philosophies to counteract the teachings of Christ. . . .

With every conceivable device he wages war with the Saints, endeavoring to make them miserable like himself, always seeking to thwart the purposes of Jehovah against whom his jealousy and resentment know no end.[33]

The War in Heaven, as set forth in the scriptures, was not merely a figurative event but was a literal occurrence with very real consequences of spiritual death and destruction. Likewise, the continuation of that conflict here on earth is every bit as real as the wars fought by mortal men and is correspondingly littered with graphic scenes of eternal spiritual carnage. Though Lucifer vainly persists in his efforts to overthrow the Father's plan, his assaults on the spirit children of the Father are not so futile. He continues to destroy agency and to lead some to believe that there is exaltation without effort and salvation without sacrifice; that good is evil, and evil good. Just as Lucifer was defeated in the premortal battleground, he will yet be bound again. By each individual, however, the battle must be won personally, on the same conditions as it was in heaven—"by the blood of the Lamb, and by the word of their testimony" (Revelation 12:11). The war continues. The dangers are the same, but so are the defenses.

> Wherefore, lift up your hearts and rejoice, and gird up your loins, and take upon you my whole armor, that ye may be able to withstand the evil day, having done all, that ye may be able to stand.
>
> Stand, therefore, having your loins girt about with truth, having on the breastplate of righteousness, and your feet shod with the preparation of the gospel of peace, which I have sent mine angels to commit unto you;
>
> Taking the shield of faith wherewith ye shall be able to quench all the fiery darts of the wicked;
>
> And take the helmet of salvation, and the sword of my Spirit, which I will pour out upon you, and my word which I reveal unto you, and be agreed as touching all things whatsoever ye ask of me, and be faithful until I come, and ye shall be caught up, that where I am ye shall be also. Amen. (D&C 27:15–18.)

Notes

1. Joseph Smith, *Teachings of the Prophet Joseph Smith* (Salt Lake City: Deseret Book Co., 1972), p. 354.

2. Bruce R. McConkie, "Who Is the Author of the Plan of Salvation?" *Improvement Era*, May 1953, p. 322.

3. Orson Pratt, in *Journal of Discourses*, 18:290.

4. The First Presidency (Joseph F. Smith, John R. Winder, Anthon H. Lund), "The Origin of Man," *Improvement Era*, November 1909, pp. 75–81; italics added.

5. First Presidency and Council of the Twelve, in *Improvement Era*, August 1916, pp. 940–941. Reprinted in James R. Clark, comp., *Messages of the First Presidency*, 6 vols. (Salt Lake City: Bookcraft, 1975), 5:33.

6. Bruce R. McConkie, *A New Witness for the Articles of Faith* (Salt Lake City: Deseret Book, 1985), p. 66.

7. Bruce R. McConkie, *The Promised Messiah* (Salt Lake City: Deseret Book Co. 1978), pp. 53–54.

8. Neal A. Maxwell, in Conference Report, October 1981, p. 9.

9. Orson F. Whitney, "Elias," as quoted in Richard H. Cracroft and Neal E. Lambert, comp., *A Believing People: Literature of the Latter-day Saints* (Salt Lake City: Bookcraft, 1974), p. 206.

10. George Q. Cannon, *Millennial Star*, 57:563–564.

11. Bruce R. McConkie, *Mormon Doctrine*, 2nd edition (Salt Lake City: Bookcraft, 1966), pp. 192–193.

12. Bruce R. McConkie, *Mormon Doctrine*, p. 744.

13. Mark E. Petersen, *The Way of the Master* (Salt Lake City: Bookcraft, 1974), p. 1.

14. Orson Pratt, in *Journal of Discourses*, 13:63.

15. Orson F. Whitney, "The Fall and the Redemption," *Improvement Era*, March 1921, p. 378.

16. J. Reuben Clark, Jr., as quoted in *Readings in Theology: A Syllabus for REL 230, "The Gospel in Principle and Practice,"* (Provo, Utah: Brigham Young University Press, 1965–1966), pp. 152–153.

17. Joseph Smith, *Teachings of the Prophet Joseph Smith*, p. 357.

18. Bruce R. McConkie, *A New Witness for the Articles of Faith*, p. 656.

19. David O. McKay, *Man May Know for Himself*, edited by Clare Middlemiss (Salt Lake City: Deseret Book Co., 1967), p. 365.

20. Orson Pratt, in *Journal of Discourses*, 21:288; italics added.

21. B. H. Roberts, "The Atonement," *The Seventy's Course in Theology*, fourth year (Salt Lake City: Deseret News, 1911), pp. 29–30; italics added.

22. Bruce R. McConkie, *A New Witness for the Articles of Faith*, p. 656.

23. Robert J. Matthews, "The Price of Redemption," *The 11th Annual Sidney B. Sperry Symposium—New Testament*, January 29, 1983 (Provo, Utah: Brigham Young University, 1983), p. 159; italics added.

24. Harold S. Kushner, *When All You've Ever Wanted Is Not Enough* (New York: Simon and Schuster, 1986), pp. 128–129.

25. Brigham Young, in *Journal of Discourses*, 13:282.

26. John Taylor, in *Journal of Discourses*, 22:299–300.

27. Brigham Young, in *Journal of Discourses*, 5:54–55.

28. See Joseph Smith, *Teachings of the Prophet Joseph Smith*, pp. 357–358.

29. Orson Pratt, *The Seer*, vol. 1, no. 4., pp. 54–55, as quoted in Robert J. Matthews, "The Price of Redemption," in *The 11th Annual Sidney B. Sperry Symposium—New Testament*, p. 160.

30. Bruce R. McConkie, *The Promised Messiah*, p. 219.

31. J. Reuben Clark, Jr., as quoted in *Readings in Theology*, pp. 152–153.

32. Wilford Woodruff, *Discourses of Wilford Woodruff*, edited by G. Homer Durham (Salt Lake City: Bookcraft, 1969), pp. 238–240.

33. Mark E. Petersen, *The Way of the Master*, pp. 2–4.

7

Called and Prepared from the Foundation of the World

With the War in Heaven finally won, two thirds of our Heavenly Father's spirit children remained in the "first estate." The others, because of their rebellion and extreme wickedness, not only were cast out of their first estate but also lost the privilege of entering the "second estate."

Among those who remained and who would yet be able to enter mortality, there was still great diversity. Not only had the spirits not been equally diligent and obedient to the laws and commandments in the premortal world but also they now had exhibited varying degrees of valiance and faithfulness in the War in Heaven as well. No doubt there were even some who had maintained a close relationship with Lucifer and who had adhered to his apostate teachings, but whose sins and rebellion were of lesser nature and thus did not warrant expulsion. There were probably some who, though they followed the Father's plan and supported the selection of Jehovah, were not necessarily committed and zealous in sustaining and defending the truths of the gospel. They were probably less inclined toward spiritual matters than those who steadfastly and with "an eye single to the glory of God" fought against Lucifer and his hellish host. As previously cited, Abraham saw in vision these spirits who remained in their first estate and saw the diversity that existed among them. "Now the Lord had shown unto me, Abraham, the intelligences that were organized before the world was; and among all these there were many of the noble and great ones; And God saw these souls that they were good, and he stood in the midst of them, and he said: These I will make my rulers; for he stood among those that were spirits, and he saw that they were good; and he said unto me: Abraham, thou art one of them; thou wast chosen before thou wast born" (Abraham 3:22–23).

Abraham learned what Jeremiah, Peter, Paul, and many others of the prophets and apostles would learn—that God, in the premortal world, chose individuals and groups of his spirit offspring and predesignated them for special responsibilities and blessings. All of these predesignations were "according to the foreknowledge of God the Father" (1 Peter 1:2). These premortal designations represent the doctrine known among Latter-day Saints as *foreordination*. Elder Bruce R. McConkie defined this doctrine as follows:

> To carry forward his own purposes among men and nations, the Lord *foreordained* chosen spirit children in pre-existence and assigned them to come to earth at particular times and places so that they might aid in furthering the divine will. These pre-existence appointments, made "according to the foreknowledge of God the Father" (1 Peter 1:2), simply designated certain individuals to perform missions which the Lord in his wisdom knew they had the talents and capacities to do.[1]

As Elder McConkie pointed out, foreordination is simply the premortal selection of individuals and/or nations to come forth in mortality at specified times and under certain conditions. Each of these selections is based on the omniscience and eternal wisdom of the Father. Although the doctrine is really rather fundamental, supported by numerous references and examples in the scriptures, the doctrine and its application to mankind have been misunderstood. The confusion results from a failure to recognize the true relationship between the *foreknowledge* of God and his *foreordinations*.

Foreordination Is Not Predestination

The scriptures clearly attest to the omniscience of God. The Apostle Paul said, "Known unto God are all his works from the beginning of the world" (Acts 15:18). Nephi also taught that "the Lord knoweth all things from the beginning; wherefore, he prepareth a way to accomplish all his works among the children of men" (1 Nephi 9:6). Nephi, son of Helaman, also taught that God "knoweth as well all things which shall befall us as he knoweth of our iniquities" (Helaman 8:8). Numerous other passages attest to the infinite knowledge of God. The Prophet Joseph Smith taught that God's ability to save his children is directly related to his omniscience: "Without the knowledge of all things, God would not be able to save any portion of his creatures; . . . and if it were not for the idea existing in the minds of men that God had all knowledge it would be impossible for them to exercise faith in him."[2]

Foreordinations are based on God's knowledge of man—of both his premortal characteristics and propensities and his ultimate course of life. The prophet Alma taught that those chosen in the premortal world to be leaders on earth were "called and prepared from the foundation of the world according to the foreknowledge of God" (Alma 13:3). The Apostle Paul also taught that premortal elections and appointments were made according to God's foreknowledge. It was Paul's use of the word *predestinate* in connection with the doctrine of election that has caused theological differences concerning the nature of God's foreknowledge and the resulting election of his children. "For whom he did foreknow, he also did predestinate to be conformed to the image of his Son, that he might be the firstborn among many brethren. Moreover whom he did predestinate, them he also called: and whom he called, them he also justified: and whom he justified, them he also glorified." (Romans 8:29–30. Note that in his inspired translation, the Prophet Joseph Smith rendered these two verses to apply specifically to Jesus Christ only. Several important words are changed. See JST Romans 8:29–30.) To the Ephesian Saints, who understood the doctrine of premortal foreordinations, Paul wrote: "According as he hath chosen us in him before the foundation of the world, that we should be holy and without blame before him in love: Having predestinated us unto the adoption of children by Jesus Christ to himself, according to the good pleasure of his will" (Ephesians 1:4–5).

In each of these passages the word *predestinate* could also be translated *foreordain* or *appoint*. In fact, the Greek word from which the King James translators chose the word *predestinate* has a variety of meanings. The emphasis in the Greek suggests the foreknowledge of God, but not in an ultimate determination of all things excluding man's agency. For this reason many Bible revisions and newer translations replace the word *predestinate* with words such as *foreordain* or *appoint*.[3]

Without an understanding of the premortal world and the doctrine of foreordination through latter-day revelation, some may understandably interpret *predestinate* and *God's foreknowledge* to mean that there is absolute determinism in all things. One theologian who came to this conclusion was John Calvin. He went beyond what Paul taught on the doctrine of election or foreordination and interpreted these passages to mean that God not only foreknew events but also actually caused them to happen. Thus, God became the causal agent, negating man's agency in the matter. With his acceptance of the doctrine of *ex nihilo* creation, it would seem natural for Calvin to conclude that predestination implied causation by God. Calvin claimed that "by predestination we mean the eternal decree of God, by which he determines with himself whatever he wished to happen with regard to every man. All are not created on equal terms, but some are preordained to eternal life, others to eternal damnation. And accordingly, as each has been created for one or the other of these ends, we say that he has been predestinated to life or to death."[4]

Thus Calvin taught that God determined in advance, according to his omniscience, who would be saved and who would be damned. Such predestination, according to Calvin, was not due to acts of individual agency or righteousness but solely due to God's foreknowledge. Elder Bruce R. McConkie characterized this doctrine as a "sectarian substitute for the true doctrine of *foreordination*."

> Just as Lucifer "sought to destroy the agency of man" in the pre-existence (Moses 4:3), so through his ministers here he has taught a doctrine, based on scriptural distortions, of salvation and damnation without choice on the part of the individual. Predestination is the false doctrine that from all eternity God has ordered whatever comes to pass, having especial and particular reference to the salvation or damnation of souls. Some souls, according to this false concept, are irrevocably chosen for salvation, others for damnation; and there is said to be nothing any individual can do to escape his predestined inheritance in heaven or in hell as the case may be. . . .
>
> It is true that the words *predestinate* and *predestinated* are found in the King James translation of some of Paul's writings, . . . but Biblical revisions use the words *foreordain* and *foreordained*, which more accurately convey Paul's views. However, even as the King James Version renders the passages, there is no intimation of any compulsion or denial of free agency, for one of the dictionary definitions of foreordination is predestination, meaning the prior appointment (in pre-existence) of particular persons to perform designated labors or gain particular rewards.[5]

While the doctrine of predestination was adopted by some Protestant denominations, there were also many who parted company with Calvin over his view of "absolute determinism." There continue to be diverse views on the relationship between God's foreknowledge and predestination. C. S. Lewis, a Christian writer and theologian, took an interesting approach to predestination when he taught that God's foreknowledge need not imply causation.

> Everyone who believes in God at all believes that He knows what you and I are going to do tomorrow. But if He knows I am going to do so-and-so, how can I be free to do otherwise? Well, here once again, the difficulty comes from thinking that God is progressing along the Time-line like us: the only difference being that He can see ahead and we cannot. Well, if that were true, if God *foresaw* our acts, it would be very hard to understand how we could be free not to do them. But suppose God is outside and above the Time-line. In that case, what we call "tomorrow" is visible to Him in just the same way as what we call "today." All the days are "Now" for Him. He does not remember you doing things yesterday; He simply sees you doing them, because, though you have lost yesterday, He has not. He does not "foresee" you doing things tomorrow; He simply sees you doing them: because, though tomorrow is not yet there for you, it is for Him. You never suppose that your actions at this moment were any less free because God knows what you are doing. Well, He knows your tomorrow's actions in just the same way—because He is already in tomorrow and can simply watch you. In a sense, He does not know your action till you have done it: but then the moment at which you have done it is already "Now" for Him.[6]

While the theological debate continues in some religious circles, modern prophets have consistently taught the true relationship between foreknowledge and agency. President Brigham Young said:

> I will here say that it is a mistaken idea, as entertained by the Calvinists, that God has decreed all things whatsoever

that come to pass, for the volition of the creature is as free as air. You may inquire whether we believe in foreordination; we do, as strongly as any people in the world. We believe that Jesus was foreordained before the foundations of the world were built, and his mission was appointed him in eternity to be the Savior of the world, yet when he came in the flesh he was left free to choose or refuse to obey his Father. Had he refused to obey his Father, he would have become a son of perdition. We also are free to choose or refuse the principles of eternal life. God has decreed and foreordained many things that have come to pass, and he will continue to do so; but when he decrees great blessings upon a nation or upon an individual they are decreed upon certain conditions.[7]

Elder James E. Talmage also taught emphatically that foreordination based on the foreknowledge of God does not imply compulsion.

The doctrine of absolute predestination, resulting in a nullification of man's free agency, has been advocated with various modifications by different sects. Nevertheless, such teachings are wholly unjustified by both the letter and the spirit of sacred writ. God's foreknowledge concerning the natures and capacities of His children enables Him to see the end of their earthly career even from the first. . . . Many people have been led to regard this foreknowledge of God as a predestination whereby souls are designated for glory or condemnation even before their birth in the flesh, and irrespective of individual merit or demerit. This heretical doctrine seeks to rob Deity of mercy, justice, and love; it would make God appear capricious and selfish, directing and creating all things solely for His own glory, caring not for the suffering of His victims. How dreadful, how inconsistent is such an idea of God! It leads to the absurd conclusion that the mere knowledge of coming events must act as a determining influence in bringing about those occurrences. God's knowledge of spiritual and of human nature enables Him to conclude with certainty as to the actions of any of His children under given conditions; yet that knowledge is not of compelling force upon the creature.[8]

It is difficult, if not impossible, to comprehend with our finite minds the nature of God's foreknowledge. We cannot help but wonder how God can know all things about us, including our ultimate destiny, and yet not interfere with our agency. Despite our limitations, it is important to recognize the interweavings of God's foreknowledge with man's agency in order to understand the scenario of premortal selection. Elder Neal A. Maxwell used the symbol of a university as an analogy to teach this difficult concept. He explained that universities can often predict with unusual levels of accuracy the future collegiate grades of an incoming freshman student. These predictions are based on certain empirical tests and careful observation of the student's past performance. Although the university may be able to predict a student's eventual output, this prediction does not compel that student or interfere with his actual academic behavior. Elder Maxwell relates this carefully calculated forecast to God's foreknowledge of our future conduct. And though, unlike the predictions from a university, God's knowledge of our future is absolute and not merely a prediction, we still must use our agency to demonstrate our faithfulness or lack of it. Elder Maxwell summarized the relationship between foreknowledge and foreordination this way:

> God, the Father, who knows us perfectly, surely can foresee how we will respond to various challenges. While we often do not rise to our opportunities, God is neither pleased nor surprised. But we cannot say to him later on that we could have achieved if we had just been given the chance! This is all part of the justice of God.
> ... When we mortals try to comprehend, rather than merely accept, foreordination, the result is one in which finite minds futilely try to comprehend omniscience. A full understanding is impossible; we simply have to trust in what the Lord has told us, knowing enough, however, to realize that we are not dealing with *guarantees* from God but extra *opportunities*—and heavier responsibilities. If those responsibilities are in some ways linked to past performance or to past capabilities, it should not surprise us.

... It should not disconcert us, therefore, that the Lord has indicated that he chose some individuals before they came here to carry out certain assignments and, hence, these individuals have been foreordained. . . .

Foreordination is like any other blessing—it is a conditional bestowal subject to our faithfulness. Prophecies foreshadow events without determining the outcomes, because of a divine foreseeing of outcomes. So foreordination is a conditional bestowal of a role, a responsibility, or a blessing which, likewise, foresees but does not fix the outcome.[9]

Our Heavenly Father, in his infinite knowledge and wisdom, has thus called and prepared many of his spirit children from the foundation of the world for important responsibilities and blessings. The fulfillment of these foreordinations is dependent upon our own faithfulness. There are several types of foreordinations. There are foreordinations of entire nations to significant blessings, and there is the foreordination of a specific individual to a very unique and important responsibility or mission. Whatever the type of foreordained mission or blessing, its realization remains contingent upon individual agency and accountability.

Foreordination to Lineages, Nations, and Families

Foreordination to the House of Israel

We most often think that foreordination applies to a premortal calling conferred upon individuals, but perhaps the most important meaning of foreordination is in reference to the blessings and responsibilities that were foreordained to an entire group. Moses spoke of this type of foreordination as he spoke of all the house of Israel. "Remember the days of old, consider the years of many generations: ask thy father, and he will shew thee; thy elders, and they will tell thee. When the most High divided to the nations their inheritance, when he separated the sons of Adam, *he set the bounds of the people according to the number of the children of Israel. For the Lord's portion is his people; Jacob is the lot of his inheritance.*" (Deuteronomy 32:7–9; italics added.)

Commenting on this Old Testament passage and its implications to the doctrine of foreordination generally and to the house of Israel specifically, President Harold B. Lee said:

> It would seem very clear, then, that . . . Jacob, who was later to be called Israel, and his posterity, who were known as the children of Israel, were born into the most illustrious lineage of any of those who came upon the earth as mortal beings.
>
> *All these rewards were seemingly promised, or foreordained, before the world was. Surely these matters must have been determined by the kind of lives we had lived in that premortal spirit world.* Some may question these assumptions, but at the same time they will accept without any question the belief that each one of us will be judged when we leave this earth according to his or her deeds during our lives here in mortality. Isn't it just as reasonable to believe that what we have received here in this earth life was given to each of us according to the merits of our conduct before we came here?[10]

Also, as previously cited, the Apostle Paul taught the doctrine of election to the Saints in Rome and Ephesus. Election, in this instance, is a type of collective foreordination—a selection of spirits to form an entire favored group or lineage. Although it is a collective foreordination it is nonetheless based on individual premortal faithfulness and spiritual capacity. Elder Melvin J. Ballard, in a classic address given in 1922 entitled "The Three Degrees of Glory," explained how some were foreordained to be of the house of Israel.

> There was a group of souls tested, tried, and proven before they were born into the world, and the Lord provided a lineage for them. That lineage is the house of Israel, the lineage of Abraham, Isaac and Jacob and their posterity. Through this lineage were to come the *true and tried souls that had demonstrated their righteousness in the spirit world*

before they came here. Our particular branch is the house of Joseph through his son Ephraim. That is the group whence shall come the majority of the candidates for celestial glory.[11]

Elder Bruce R. McConkie further explained:

> All men are the spirit children of the Eternal Father; all dwelt in his presence, awaiting the day of their mortal probation; all have come or will come to earth at an appointed time, in a specified place, to live among a designated people. In all of this there is no chance. A divine providence rules over the nations and governs in the affairs of men. Birth and death and mortal kinship are the Lord's doings. He alone determines where and when and among what people his spirit children shall undergo their mortal probation. . . .
>
> All of these things operate by law; they are the outgrowth of long years of personal preparation in preexistence on the part of each individual; they come to pass according to the laws that the Lord has ordained. This second estate is a continuation of our first estate; we are born here with the talents and capacities acquired there. Abraham was one of the noble and great spirits in the premortal life. He was chosen for his mortal ministry and position before he was born, and as with the father of the faithful, so with all of the spirits destined to be born as his seed.
>
> The greatest and most important talent or capacity that any of the spirit children of the Father could gain is the talent of spirituality. Most of those who gained this talent were chosen, before they were born, to come to earth as members of the house of Israel. They were foreordained to receive the blessings that the Lord promised to Abraham and to his seed in all their generations. *This foreordination is an election, Paul tells us, and truly it is so, for those so chosen, selected, or elected become, in this life, the favored people. Though all mankind may be saved by obedience, some find it easier to believe and obey than others.*[12]

The doctrine of the election of Israel, or its foreordination to certain blessings, is a major though often misunderstood theme of Paul in the New Testament. It appears that this foreordination to birthright blessings in the house of Israel is a more significant foreordination than the more frequently cited examples of preappointment to specific Church callings. As Elder McConkie stated, premortal inclinations make some more believing and spiritual in mortality and thus more likely to accept the blessings and responsibilities of being members of the Church and of the house of Israel. This concept gives greater meaning to the Savior's statement that his sheep know his voice and will follow him (see John 10:4–5, 14). Once again, this foreordination does not predestinate or guarantee their acceptance of the gospel or their admission into the earthly kingdom of God. They must accept the earthly responsibilities of the house of Israel through their mortal agency as well. Yet their recognition of the familiar strains of the gospel message and their acceptance of gospel ordinances may come easier by virtue of their foreordination to the house of Israel. "Thus, when we now say 'I know,'" said Elder Neal A. Maxwell, "that realization is rediscovery; we are actually saying 'I know—again!' From long experience, His sheep know His voice and His doctrine."[13] Elder Parley P. Pratt also spoke of the significance of this premortal election or foreordination to the house of Israel.

> . . . When [God] speaks of nobility, He simply means an election made, and an office or a title conferred, on the principle of superiority of intellect, or nobleness of action, or of capacity to act. And when this election, with its titles, dignities, and estates, includes the unborn posterity of a chosen man, as in the case of Abraham, Isaac, and Jacob, it is with a view of the noble spirits of the eternal world coming through their lineage, and being taught in the commandments of God.[14]

In addition to the far-reaching foreordination to the lineage of Abraham, Isaac, and Jacob, there is yet another, more specific aspect of this foreordination spoken of in the scriptures: to be "a chosen generation, a royal priesthood, an holy nation, a peculiar people" (1 Peter 2:9; see also Exodus 19:5–6; Leviticus 20:22–26). Paul taught, "They are not all

Israel, which are of Israel" (Romans 9:6). Paul was teaching that lineage did not insure salvation. Rather, acceptance of and obedience to the principles and ordinances of the gospel were more important qualifications for being "of Israel." To become a covenant people, Paul taught that each one must accept the Mediator of the Covenant—Jesus Christ (see Hebrews 8 and 9). It appears that among the foreordained lineage of Israel, those who were covenant Israel were also foreordained to "all spiritual blessings in heavenly places in Christ" (Ephesians 1:3), and to "the adoption, and the glory, and the covenants, and the giving of the law, and the service of God, and the promises" (Romans 9:4). In light of Paul's teachings, then, the most important aspect of this foreordination to the house of Israel was the accompanying foreordination to the ordinances of salvation and the spiritual blessings attending membership in the earthly kingdom of God. Of these foreordained spiritual blessings and ordinances Elder Bruce R. McConkie wrote:

> All Israel, according to the doctrine of foreordination, have it in their power to gain exaltation; to be like the Son of God, having gained his image; to be joint-heirs with him; to be justified and glorified; to be adopted into the family of God by faith; to be participators with their fathers in the covenant that God made with them; and to be inheritors, to the full, of the ancient promises. Implicit in all this is the fact that they are foreordained to be baptized, to join the Church, to receive the priesthood, to enter the ordinance of celestial marriage, and to be sealed up unto eternal life.[15]

It is certainly not to be thought that those spirits who were less faithful in the premortal world and were not foreordained to the blessings of the house of Israel have no chance on earth to yet gain those blessings and ultimately qualify for eternal life. Elder Alvin R. Dyer wrote:

> Members of The Church of Jesus Christ of Latter-day Saints have come to know by divine revelation in our modern time the importance of the house of Israel and its re-

lationship to the plan of the gospel. They have come to know that the house of Israel represents the chosen of the Lord. There *is* a chosen people—there *is* a royal lineage among men here upon the earth. Many are born into it by virtue of their pre-mortal worthiness, and others may obtain it through adoption, by virtue of accepting the gospel here in mortality.[16]

This foreordination was the natural consequence or blessing for premortal compliance with eternal laws. Joseph Smith taught: "There is a law, irrevocably decreed in heaven before the foundations of this world, upon which all blessings are predicated—And when we obtain any blessing from God, it is by obedience to that law upon which it is predicated" (D&C 130:20–21). Elder McConkie explained that the blessing for those "elected" there was that "it is easier for them to believe the gospel than it is for the generality of mankind." He went on to say, "Every living soul comes into this world with sufficient talent to believe and be saved, but the Lord's sheep, as a reward for their devotion when they dwelt in his presence, enjoy greater spiritual endowments than their fellows."[17]

The scriptures proclaim that all mankind are commanded, expected, and able to abide the principles of salvation. The Lord taught Alma that "all mankind, yea, men and women, all nations, kindreds, tongues and people, must be born again; yea, born of God, changed from their carnal and fallen state, to a state of righteousness, being redeemed of God, becoming his sons and daughters; And thus they become new creatures; and unless they do this, they can in nowise inherit the kingdom of God" (Mosiah 27:25–26; see also 2 Nephi 26:33; Moses 6:52–57). While the commandment is the same for all mankind in all ages of eternity, those spirits who developed greater predispositions for righteousness were rewarded with "the believing blood of Israel" and become foreordained heirs to the blessings associated with the favored lineage.

This inclination toward spirituality may make it easier for them to recognize the gospel message, but it does not preclude others from also repenting and receiving an inheritance in the house of Israel. These others, through their earthly faithfulness, become, as Paul taught, "adopted" into the favored lineage—receiving all of the blessings and responsibilities to which they are entitled—and their apparent lack of a premortal foreordination is overcome when they become *as though* they had been foreordained. In the Abrahamic covenant the Lord promises, "For as many as receive this Gospel shall be called after thy name, and shall be accounted thy seed, and shall rise up and bless thee, as their father" (Abraham 2:10). This seems to open the door for any who can qualify. The scriptures are replete with invitations to all to partake of his salvation. Nephi reasons, "Behold, hath the Lord commanded any that they should not partake of his goodness? Behold I say unto you, Nay; but all men are privileged the one like unto the other, and none are forbidden." (2 Nephi 26:28.) On the other hand, the premortal foreordination of a spirit to the house of Israel with its attendant blessings becomes effective only as that spirit obediently and faithfully responds to the earthly laws and ordinances of the gospel. Elder Dallin H. Oaks wrote:

> What does it mean to be an "heir" of the celestial kingdom? An heir is one who has a rightful claim to an inheritance. But his inheritance is not automatic. An heir must perfect his claim by complying with certain formalities. In the secular law, these formalities include such requirements as filing a proof of heirship within the required time and showing that all the debts of the estate are paid. In the gospel law, the formalities include the required ordinances of the gospel.[18]

To the Prophet Joseph Smith the Lord reiterated that righteousness and obedience, not merely foreordination and lineage, are required in order for one to truly be of "covenant Israel." "For, verily I say that the rebellious are not of the blood of Ephraim" (D&C 64:36). Many may be born into the house of Israel on the basis of a premortal foreordination, but many may still lose the covenant blessings through rebellion.

Foreordination to Nations of the Earth

In addition to foreordination to the lineage of Israel, there is also a premortal designation as to both the time and place of our birth which constitutes a foreordination. Teaching the Athenian intellectuals on Mars' hill, the Apostle Paul explained, "God that made the world and all things therein . . . hath made of one blood all nations of men for to dwell on all the face of the earth, and hath determined the times before appointed, and the bounds of their habitation" (Acts 17:24, 26). Elder Bruce R. McConkie, commenting on Paul's statement, explained how our place and time in mortality was foreordained. "God sends his spirit children to earth on a regular, organized schedule. There is nothing haphazard or accidental about the peopling of the earth or the assignment of various land areas to the races of men. The race and nation in which men are born in this world is a direct result of their pre-existent life. All the spirit hosts of heaven deemed worthy to receive mortal bodies were foreordained to pass through this earthly probation in the particular race and nation suited to their needs, circumstances, and talents."[19]

The Father's foreordination of his spirit children to the various nations of the earth was based on three fundamental principles. First, as is always the case, foreordination comes as a blessing or reward for premortal righteousness and valiance. President Harold B. Lee said that we have come into mortality to specific nations "as a reward for the kind of lives [we] lived before [we] came here."[20] President David O. McKay also stated that our lineage was predetermined not only by premortal faithfulness, but also by premortal attraction.

Now if none of these spirits were permitted to enter mortality until they all were good and great and had become leaders, then the diversity of conditions among the children of men as we see them today would certainly seem to indicate discrimination and injustice. But if in their eagerness to take upon themselves bodies, the spirits were willing to come through any lineage for which they were worthy, or to which they were attracted, then they were given the full reward of merit, and were satisfied, yes, and even blessed.

. . . Our place in this world would then be determined by our own advancement or condition in the premortal state, just as our place in our future existence will be determined by what we do here in mortality.[21]

President McKay indicates that closely associated with the premortal faithfulness or lack of it in individual spirits is their attraction to other spirits or groups of spirits of like character. This view and its relationship to foreordination to specific lineages and nations is based on the principle of "spiritual attraction" described by the Lord in modern revelation. "For intelligence cleaveth unto intelligence; wisdom receiveth wisdom; truth embraceth truth; virtue loveth virtue; light cleaveth unto light; mercy hath compassion on mercy and claimeth her own; justice continueth its course and claimeth its own" (D&C 88:40).

Second, the placement into certain nations was done by an infinitely wise and compassionate Father for the good of each of his children. No doubt each spirit child was assigned to such a nation as would be best for his or her own growth and development. This principle is reflected in the following statement of Elder Alvin R. Dyer:

The very nature of each person . . . would require that the lineage of birth would fit the caliber of their person; this, no doubt, entailed a birth into mortality by pre-mortal judgment. Equality of birth is not actually possible, because there is no equality of all spirit persons. Thus to bring about birth into mortality there must have been a plan to calibrate birth in a lineage and manner best suited to the need of potential growth and development in the Second Estate, which is a probationary period. . . .

In consequence of this, in order for man to come from pre-mortality into mortality, there is a foreordination or assignment . . . associated with a judgment and assignment to that division to which they are best suited and can make the more effective progress within that realm.[22]

The third principle that must be emphasized in any discussion of foreordination is that God designates individual spirits to come into mortality through specific nations, races, and cultures at specific times in the world's history to bring to pass his works and to fulfil his plans for all mankind. These plans not only include the salvation of his individual children but also encompass deeds and teachings designed to elevate mankind. Great spirits have come to all nations and races to render service to humanity and contribute to the enlightenment of others. "The great religious leaders of the world," wrote the First Presidency, "such as Mohammed, Confucius, and the Reformers, as well as philosophers including Socrates, Plato, and others received a portion of God's light. Moral truths were given to them by God to enlighten whole nations and to bring a higher level of understanding to individuals."[23] Thousands of other great and noble spirits, who were not as famous but whose service and compassion have been significant, have been and will continue to be sent to all the nations of the earth. Elder Erastus Snow taught of these noble spirits:

They have been first and foremost in everything noble among men in the various nations in breaking off the shackles of kingcraft and priestcraft and oppression of every kind, and the foremost among men in upholding and maintaining the principles of liberty and freedom . . . whose efforts are directed in establishing upon the earth those heaven-born principles which tend directly to blessing and salvation, to ameliorating the condition of their fellow-men, and elevating them in the scale of their being.[24]

There is no random assignment or chance in these predesignations. Foreordination to the various nations of the earth comes not only as a reward for faithfulness or as an opportunity for individual growth and service but also—and perhaps even more important—as a way to further the works and designs of God for his spirit children. The prophet Alma taught his son Helaman "that by small and simple things are great things brought to pass. . . . And the Lord God doth work by means to bring about his great and eternal purposes; and by very small means the Lord doth confound the wise and bringeth about the salvation of many souls" (Alma 37:6–7). Later, Alma taught another son, Corianton, that "God bringeth about his great and eternal purposes, which were prepared from the foundation of the world" (Alma 42:26). So it is also with God's foreordinations of his children. Predesignations and assignments to the nations of the earth are a major factor in bringing about the Father's "great and eternal purposes" designed to bless the lives of his children, bring them happiness, and "bring to pass the immortality and eternal life of man" (Moses 1:39).

The times, places, and circumstances of our birth into mortality could be determined by any or all of these factors. While we may understand the general principles behind such foreordinations, it is impossible to know which factor or combination of factors applies in each individual case. Therefore we must never attempt to judge an individual's premortal character based on his national origin, race, cultural background, or circumstances in life. We must keep in mind that our Heavenly Father has sent "noble and great ones" to the earth under many circumstances and to virtually all the nations of the earth. Abraham was born in the paganistic society of Ur, where the people's "hearts were set to do evil" and where children were offered as sacrifices to "dumb idols" (Abraham 1:1–7). Moses was born in bondage and raised in the household of a murderous, infidel Egyptian pharaoh. Numerous other examples are found in the scriptures. Even in the latter days, many of those noble and great spirits whom the Lord foreordained to be his "rulers" have been born in diverse racial and cultural backgrounds. They have come into poverty and obscurity and into unbelieving families as well as into situations of faith and freedom, prosperity and prominence. Some of the Father's choicest spirits are born in huts and hogans.

Paul taught that God appointed or foreordained not only the "bounds of their habitation" but also the times. Each of the principles previously discussed also applies to our appointed time of birth into mortality. While it is obvious that God has sent worthy and faithful spirits into mortality in every dispensation, the prophets have taught that God has also reserved many of his choice spirits to come forth in the tumultuous times of the last days. Iniquity abounds as Lucifer's "last-gasp" evil efforts increase and the need for righteous and worthy spirits to carry forth God's purposes and designs increases proportionately. President Wilford Woodruff said, "The Lord has chosen a small number of choice spirits of Sons and Daughters out of all the creations of God, who are to inherit the earth, and the company of choice spirits have been kept in the Spirit World for 6,000 years, to come forth in the last days, to stand in the flesh in the last dispensation of the fulness of times, to organize the Kingdom of God upon the earth, to build it up and to defend it."[25]

Many years later, two other latter-day prophets, echoing President Woodruff's sentiments, made statements regarding the foreordination of the youth of the Church who would come forth in these last days. President Joseph Fielding Smith observed that "our young people are among the most blessed and favored of our Father's children. They are the nobility of heaven, a choice and chosen generation who have a divine destiny. Their spirits have been reserved to come forth in this day when the Gospel is on the earth, and when the Lord needs valiant servants to carry on His great latter-day work."[26] President Harold B. Lee also reminded the youth of their foreordained place in the history of the world. "You our youth of today are among the most illustrious spirits to be born into mortality in any age of the world. Yours is a noble heritage and a wonderful opportunity."[27] In 1980, President Ezra Taft Benson delivered this motivating message to the students of Brigham Young University:

> For nearly six thousand years, God has held you in reserve to make your appearance in the final days before the Second Coming of the Lord. Every previous gospel dispensation has drifted into apostasy, but ours will not. . . . God has saved for the final inning some of his strongest children, who will help bear off the Kingdom triumphantly. And that is where you come in, for you are the generation that must be prepared to meet your God.
>
> All through the ages the prophets have looked down through the corridors of time to our day. Billions of the deceased and those yet to be born have their eyes on us. Make no mistake about it—you are a marked generation. There has never been more expected of the faithful in such a short period of time as there is of us. Never before on the face of this earth have the forces of evil and the forces of good been as well organized. . . .
>
> . . . Each day we personally make many decisions that show where our support will go. The final outcome is certain—the forces of righteousness will finally win. What remains to be seen is where each of us personally, now and in the future, will stand in this fight—and how tall we will stand. Will we be true to our last-days, foreordained mission?[28]

Foreordination to Favored Families

Perhaps no other institution or influence can shape our character or prepare us for life more than the family. It is for this reason that families are an important aspect of the doctrine of foreordination. The family unit is paramount in God's designs. Elder Bruce R. McConkie stated that "the Lord operates through families. He himself lives in the family unit; it is his eternal system of government in heaven and on earth, and he always offers as much of his own system to men as they are willing to receive."[29] In addition to foreordination to lineage, there is evidence to indicate that there is, at least in certain cases, foreordination to favored families. President Harold B. Lee affirmed that, generally, we come to certain families as a reward or blessing for our premortal lives.[30] Undoubtedly, premortal assignment to specific families is based also on what is best for individual and familial growth and development and what will best further the works and purposes of God.

This foreordination to families is best illustrated in the noble heritage of the latter-day prophets from Joseph Smith to Ezra Taft Benson. Each was prepared for his monumental ministry from the cradle at the fireside of a favored and faithful family. President Brigham Young spoke of the importance of the parentage of Joseph Smith in preparing Joseph for his foreordained prophetic mantle.

> It was decreed in the counsels of eternity, long before the foundations of the earth were laid, that he should be the man, in the last dispensation of this world, to bring forth the word of God to the people, and receive the fulness of the keys and power of the Priesthood of the Son of God. The Lord had his eye upon him, and upon his father, and upon his father's father, and upon their progenitors clear back to Abraham, and from Abraham to the flood, from the flood to Enoch, and from Enoch to Adam. He has watched that family and that blood as it has circulated from its fountain to the birth of that man.

On the day that Spencer W. Kimball was sustained as prophet and President of the Church, Elder Bruce R. Mc-Conkie similarly remarked:

> May I take President Spencer W. Kimball as an illustration and pattern of one who was prepared, foreordained, and called to leadership among the Lord's people. He was, it is true, born in the household of faith. . . .

But more than mortal birth . . . [is] involved. He was born in the household of faith for a reason. . . . The fact is, he is a spirit son of God who was called and chosen and foreordained before the foundations of the earth were laid, and he is now fulfilling the destiny designed for him from the preexistence.[32]

As important as families are in the great plan of happiness and redemption, it seems unlikely that foreordination to favored families would be limited to prophets. It has not been revealed, however, to what extent this foreordination applies. We can assume with confidence that some predesignation to families took place, but again we must be extremely careful in trying to ascribe this principle of foreordination to specific individuals and families. Responding to one particular inquiry from a Latter-day Saint woman, Elder John Taylor published an article entitled "The Origin and Destiny of Woman" in the August 29, 1857 edition of *The Mormon*. In this response he advanced the notion that, at least in some specific cases, we chose in the premortal life those who would be our earthly parents, spouses, and even children. "You also chose a kindred spirit whom you loved in the spirit world (and who had permission to come to this planet and take a tabernacle), to be your head, stay, husband and protector on the earth and to exalt you in eternal worlds. All these were arranged, likewise the spirits that should tabernacle through your lineage."[33] The difficulty with this statement, however, is knowing how far Elder Taylor intended the principle to be applied. The question remains—Did this reference to a premortal choice of companion and family apply specifically to the woman who inquired, or was Elder Taylor teaching a broader application of the principle?

While there is evidence of at least some degree of foreordination to families, President Joseph Fielding Smith taught that there was "no scriptural justification . . . for the belief that we had the privilege of choosing our parents and our life companions in the spirit world."[34] Addressing this issue in a talk given to seminary and institute teachers in 1966, Elder Harold B. Lee stated that "we have no revealed word" on the extent to which premortal choices of family members were made. He then cautioned that we should not accept or teach ideas that cannot be firmly established in the standard works or by inspired utterances of the living prophets. In 1971, the First Presidency once again declared that "we have no re- vealed word to the effect that when we were in the preexis- tent state we chose our parents and our husbands and wives."[35]

Because of the eternal significance of marriage and fami- lies, it is reasonable to assume that there may have been some covenants or choices made in the premortal life and also that special divine guidance may be given here on earth. How- ever, it is important to remember that this may not apply to all of God's children. As President Joseph Fielding Smith stated: "This belief has been advocated by some, and it is possible that in some instances it is true, but it would require too great a stretch of the imagination to believe it to be so in all, or even in the majority of cases. Most likely we came where those in authority decided to send us. Our agency may not have been exercised to the extent of making choice of parents and posterity."[36]

Foreordination to favored families may come as a reward for premortal righteousness, but, perhaps more important, such foreordination is based on what will best correspond to the capacities of the individual, provide him or his family with optimal opportunities for growth and service, and fulfill the designs and purposes of God. We must remember that our Heavenly Father often sends some of his noble and great spirits to the least likely families because he knows that they have the spiritual capacities to rise above those conditions and, in turn, bring blessings to that entire family. As the Lord taught Isaiah, "For my thoughts are not your thoughts, neither are your ways my ways. . . . For as the heavens are higher than the earth, so are my ways higher than your ways, and my thoughts than your thoughts." (Isaiah 55:8–9.) It is for this reason that we must never attempt to judge someone's premortal character or performance based on parentage or family conditions. While it is true that we believe in the *general* concept of foreordination to favored families, we do not fully understand its *specific* application to individual cases. Until more is revealed we are as Paul said: "For now we see through a glass, darkly; but then face to face: now I know in part; but then shall I know even as also I am known" (1 Corinthians 13:12).

Foreordination to Priesthood Callings

Among those foreordained to the house of Israel were those who were further ordained to specific callings as ministers in the kingdom of God. The Prophet Joseph Smith taught that "every man who has a calling to minister to the inhabitants of the world was ordained to that very purpose in the Grand Council of heaven before this world was. I suppose that I was ordained to this very office in that Grand Council."[37] Abraham understood this principle and saw its operation in his vision. "Now the Lord had shown unto me, Abraham, the intelligences that were organized before the world was; and among all these there were many of the noble and great ones; And God saw these souls that they were good, and he stood in the midst of them, and he said: *These I will make my rulers;* for he stood among those that were spirits, and he saw that they were good; and he said unto me: Abraham, thou art one of them; thou wast chosen before thou wast born" (Abraham 3:22–23; italics added).

Abraham and these noble and great spirits were not foreordained to be "rulers" in the sense of being monarchs, heads of nations, or leaders in a governmental or political sense, but rather to be spiritual leaders in the kingdom of God on earth. To Jeremiah the Lord said: "Before I formed thee in the belly I knew thee; and before thou camest forth out of the womb I sanctified thee, and I ordained thee a prophet unto the nations" (Jeremiah 1:5). The great prototype for all priesthood foreordinations is the Savior himself. He was fore-ordained in the premortal councils to the greatest of all ministries on earth and to the most significant service ever rendered to the family of God. The Apostle Peter referred to Christ as "a lamb without blemish and without spot: Who verily was foreordained before the foundation of the world" (1 Peter 1:19–20). All other priesthood foreordinations were patterned after his, and all those thus foreordained were to bear witness of and bring men to that Lamb who was slain from before the foundation of the earth. President Wilford Woodruff declared, "In every dispensation the Lord has had those who were fore-ordained to do a certain work. We all dwelt in the presence of God before we came here, and such men as Abraham, Isaac, Jacob, the ancient Prophets, Jesus and the Apostles received their appointments before the world was made. They were ordained before the foundation of the world to come and tabernacle here in the flesh and to work for the cause of God, and this because of their faith and faithfulness."[38]

Foreordination to priesthood assignments was not reserved solely for heads of dispensations or for prophets, ancient or modern. Numerous other noble and great spirit sons of God were likewise foreordained to "minister to the inhabitants of the world" and render priesthood service of eternal consequence. President John Taylor noted that "there are thousands of men upon the earth to-day, among the Saints of God, of whom it was decreed before they came that they should occupy the positions they have occupied and do occupy, and many of them have performed their part and gone home; others are left to still fulfill the duties and responsibilities devolving upon them."[39]

Foreordination to a priesthood assignment involves much more than just a premortal calling to be a prophet, Apostle, General Authority, stake president, or bishop. Relatively few of God's sons were foreordained to become prophets or apostles, but all those who receive the Melchizedek Priesthood in mortality were foreordained. The prophet Alma taught that holders of the high priesthood were *"called and prepared from the foundation of the world* according to the foreknowledge of God, on account of their exceeding faith and good works; in the first place being left to choose good or evil; therefore they having chosen good, and exercising exceedingly great faith, are called with a holy calling . . . this holy calling *being prepared from the foundation of the world.* . . . This high priesthood being after the order of his Son, which order was from the foundation of the world; or in other words, being without beginning of days or end of years, being prepared from eternity to all eternity, according to his foreknowledge of all things" (Alma 13:3, 5, 7; italics added).

Sometimes we may lose sight of the fact that these special priesthood foreordinations were not given just to a few prophets, but to all who, through their premortal faithfulness and diligence, would be called on earth to priesthood service. President Wilford Woodruff reminded us of the significance of these priesthood foreordinations. He spoke of the pre-earth appointments of Joseph Smith and Jeremiah who came forth in the Lord's due time to establish his work on earth. Then he continued, "And so it is the case with tens of thousands of the Elders of Israel. The Lord Almighty has conferred upon you the Holy Priesthood and made you the instrument in His hands to build up this kingdom. Do we contemplate these things as fully as we ought? Do we realize that the eyes of all the heavenly hosts are over us? Then let us do our duty."[40]

Foreordination to Special Missions in Mortality

There is another type of foreordination which Elder Neal A. Maxwell labeled "foredesignation" to distinguish it from a priesthood ordination.[41] Mary, the mortal mother of Jesus, is an example of one who was foredesignated to a significant and sacred mission in life (see 1 Nephi 11:18). Many other women through the ages and throughout the nations of the earth have shaped the history of the world and furthered the works of God through their service to their families, the Church, and society. Surely many righteous daughters of God were foredesignated to missions of secular as well as spiritual significance. Though not ordained to priesthood callings, their foredesignations to such vital missions in mortality are no less important. President Spencer W. Kimball emphasized that "we had full equality as his spirit children. We have equality as recipients of God's perfected love for each of us. . . . Within those great assurances, however, our roles and assignments differ. These are eternal differences. . . . Remember, in the world before we came here, faithful women were given certain assignments while faithful men were foreordained to certain priesthood tasks. While we do not now remember the particulars, this does not alter the glorious reality of what we once agreed to."[42]

In addition to applying to faithful women, the principle of foredesignation would likewise apply to men who, though not holders of the priesthood nor members of the kingdom of God on earth, were designated to fulfill special missions and assignments in mortality. This foredesignation of certain men and women was based on talents and abilities acquired premortally that would enable them to further God's work on earth. The prophet Isaiah identified Cyrus of Persia as one thus foredesignated to a special work. Isaiah prophesied of that important mission almost two hundred years before the birth of Cyrus (see Isaiah 44:28; 45:1). Others so foredesignated were seen in vision by Nephi. These include Columbus and other great explorers (see 1 Nephi 13:12), the pilgrim founders of America (see 1 Nephi 13:13–16), and those patriots who framed the American constitution and founded a government that would make it possible for the gospel to be restored in the last days (see 1 Nephi 13:17–19). These men, identified in the scriptures, were "called and prepared" and "raised up" by the Lord for these important missions in mortality. It is only logical to assume that much of that preparation was done premortally. President Joseph F. Smith taught that Christ "was the inspirer of the ancient philosophers, Pagan or Israelite, as well as of the great characters of modern times. Columbus, in discovery; Washington, in the struggle for freedom; Lincoln, in emancipation and union; Bacon, in philosophy; Franklin, in statesmanship and diplomacy; Stephenson, in steam; Watts, in song; [and] Edison, in electricity . . . found in Christ the source of their wisdom and the marvelous truths which they advocated." He went on to add that "Calvin, Luther, Melanchthon, and all the reformers," were inspired in doing what they did "for the amelioration, liberty and advancement of the human race. They paved the way for the more perfect gospel of truth to come."[43] No doubt there were numerous other eminent men who, though not priesthood holders, were uniquely qualified and thus, premortally foredesignated to significant missions.[44] Likewise, even today, we are the beneficiaries of significant service to humanity rendered by honorable men and women with unique talents and qualifications. Elder M. Russell Ballard has suggested that modern technological inventions and innovations "have been inspired and created for the building of the kingdom of God. If others use them, that's fine, but their basic purpose is to help spread the gospel."[45] It may be that great inventors, scientists, academicians, philosophers, and others, both in and out of the kingdom of God on earth, were also foredesignated to perform such great works on earth as to further God's "work and glory" and to bless humanity.

The fulfillment of these foreordinations and predesignations, whether they be to lineages, nations, families, priesthood callings, or to special missions in life, is dependent upon faithfulness and diligence on earth. As Elder Bruce R.

McConkie stated, "All of the Lord's work is planned and prepared in advance, and those who are called and chosen to do the work receive their commission and ordination from him, first in the preexistence and then, if they remain true and faithful, again here in mortality."[46]

Fulfilling Our Foreordinations

We may not recognize in this lifetime all of our foreordinations. There may be glimpses given in patriarchal blessings and other inspired statements. We may even experience what Elder Neal A. Maxwell described as "sudden surges of *déjà vu*" wherein intuition and intimations from beyond the veil remind us of who we were and who we may become. It is not as important to identify our specific foreordinations as it is to live in such a manner that the Lord may lead us to fulfill those premortal designations. "Foreordination is like any other blessing," said Elder Maxwell. "It is a conditional bestowal subject to our faithfulness."[47]

In the October 1973 general conference, President Harold B. Lee utilized Doctrine and Covenants 121:34–36 to illustrate the point that earthly faithfulness is required for fulfillment of premortal foreordinations. He taught that "many are called [foreordained], but few are chosen [foreordination fulfilled]." The revelation then asks, "And why are they not chosen?" In other words, why are some premortally foreordained and yet fail on earth to live up to the blessings, responsibilities, and missions that were conferred upon them? The scripture, President Lee explained, suggests two answers —first, "Because their hearts are set so much upon the things of this world," and second, because they "aspire to the honors of men" (D&C 121:35).[48] This revelation is true for principles of priesthood power on earth, and it also teaches us that foreordinations can be fulfilled "only upon the principles of righteousness" (D&C 121:36). There are many, as the

Lord stated, that fail to measure up to their premortal potential and foreordinations because of improper priorities and impure motives. Elder Neal A. Maxwell has also reminded us that "just because we were chosen 'there and then,' surely does not mean we can be indifferent 'here and now.' . . . Those called and prepared must also prove 'chosen, and faithful.' (See Rev. 17:14; D&C 121:34–36.)"[49]

The doctrine of foreordination carries with it heavy responsibilities. We cannot neglect those responsibilities but must be constantly vigilant in living so that our foreordinations, whatever they may be, can be fulfilled and God's work may be furthered. President Wilford Woodruff counselled:

> We have been raised up of the Lord to take this kingdom and bear it off. This is our duty; but if we neglect our duty and set our hearts upon the things of this world, we will be sorry for it. We ought to understand the responsibility that rests upon us. We should gird up our loins and put on the whole armor of God. . . . Then let us do our duty. Let us keep the commandments of God, let us be faithful to the end, so that when we go into the spirit world and look back upon our history we may be satisfied.[50]

As the Church continues its phenomenal growth in the last days, we stand as witnesses of the fulfilling of Nebuchadnezzar's dream that the gospel would "roll forth unto the ends of the earth, as the stone which is cut out of the mountain without hands shall roll forth, until it has filled the whole earth" (D&C 65:2; see also Daniel 2:31–45). We cannot stand on the sidelines of life and merely watch the marvelous unfolding of God's designs. We were not foreordained to be spectators but rather participants in the spectacular scenes of the last days. Lucifer's war of wickedness and efforts to destroy the plan increase proportionately to the spiritual growth and strength of the Church. The "noble and great ones" who were reserved for this day are being tested and tempted. Satan is seeking to shake us from the service which we were foreordained to perform in these most crucial yet perilous times. We must follow the counsel of the living prophets to carefully cultivate those characteristics that will enable us to fulfill our foreordained missions. Speaking to students at Brigham Young University, Elder M. Russell Ballard gave this wise counsel that is relevant to all, regardless of age or station in life:

> Do not let one day go by . . . when you do not demonstrate to the Lord that you are reliable, that you are trustworthy, that you are dedicated, . . . that you are on his side, for he is getting acquainted with the young men and the young women of this Church today. . . . Every day of your life he gets acquainted. Then, after he has watched you and after you have demonstrated your faithfulness by your service and by your ability to keep your priorities straight in your life, along comes a need for a high councilor, a Primary president, a Relief Society president, a bishop, or a stake president; and the Lord makes it known to the responsible priesthood leader that you are ready because you have lived up to the commitments and promises that you made before you were ever born.
>
> . . . I would not be a bit surprised if many of you who are sitting here would be sitting in stake presidencies, in bishoprics, in stake leadership assignments, on high councils, and, yes, there may even be one of you or more sitting in the general councils of the Church. You will only sit there, you will only receive the call, if you are ready. . . .
>
> Resolve what you have to do to be better and leave . . . with this commitment: "Heavenly Father, I will be ready in every way—spiritually, physically, emotionally—for whatever it is that thou wouldst have me do in the building of thy Kingdom on the earth."[51]

An understanding of the doctrine of foreordination can enrich our vision and increase our incentive. However, greater blessings of glory and joy await those who not only *know* the doctrine, but who *do* the works of righteousness (see John 13:17).

Notes

1. Bruce R. McConkie, *Mormon Doctrine*, 2nd edition (Salt Lake City: Bookcraft, 1966), p. 290.

2. Joseph Smith, *Lectures on Faith*, compiled by N.B. Lundwall (Salt Lake City: N.B. Lundwall, n.d.), Lecture 4, p. 43.

3. See Richard Lloyd Anderson, *Understanding Paul* (Salt Lake City: Deseret Book, Co. 1983), pp. 188–193, 262–263. Definitions from the original Greek are found in *A Greek-English Lexicon of the New Testament*, edited by William F. Arndt and F. Wilbur Gingrich (Chicago: University of Chicago Press, 1957) and *Theological Dictionary of the New Testament*, edited by Gerhard Kittel and Gerhard Friedrich, 10 vols. (Grand Rapids, Michigan: Eerdmans Publishing Co., 1967), vol. 5, p. 456. For an extensive discussion of the translation problem associated with Paul's usage of the word "predestinate," see Richard L. Anderson, "Misleading Translations of Paul," in *The 11th Annual Sidney B. Sperry Symposium — New Testament* (Provo, Utah: Religious Studies Center, Brigham Young University, 1983), pp. 17–26.

4. John Calvin, *Institutes of the Christian Religion*, translated by Henry Beveridge (Grand Rapids, Michigan: Eerdmans Publishing Co., 1979), 3, 21, 5.

5. Bruce R. McConkie, *Mormon Doctrine*, pp. 588–589.

6. C. S. Lewis, *Mere Christianity* (New York: Macmillan Publishing Co., 1952), pp. 148–149.

7. Brigham Young, in *Journal of Discourses*, 10:324.

8. James E. Talmage, *The Articles of Faith* (Salt Lake City: The Church of Jesus Christ of Latter-day Saints, 1977), p. 191. For an additional discussion of the role of God's foreknowledge, see James E. Talmage, *The Great Apostasy* (Salt Lake City: Deseret Book Co., 1953), pp. 19–20.

9. Neal A. Maxwell, "Meeting the Challenges of Today," *Speeches of the Year* (Provo, Utah: Brigham Young University, 1978), pp. 152, 154.

10. Harold B. Lee, "Understanding Who We Are Brings Self-Respect," *Ensign*, January 1974, p. 5; italics added.

11. Melvin J. Ballard, "The Three Degrees of Glory," as cited in *Melvin J. Ballard—Crusader of Righteousness* (Salt Lake City: Bookcraft, 1966), pp. 218–219; italics added.

12. Bruce R. McConkie, *A New Witness for the Articles of Faith* (Salt Lake City: Deseret Book Co., 1985), pp. 512–513; italics added.

13. Neal A. Maxwell, in Conference Report, October 1985, p. 22.

14. Parley P. Pratt, in *Journal of Discourses*, 1:258–259.

15. Bruce R. McConkie, *A New Witness for the Articles of Faith*, p. 513.

16. Alvin R. Dyer, *The Meaning of Truth* (Salt Lake City: Deseret Book Co., 1961), p. 19.

17. Bruce R. McConkie, *A New Witness for the Articles of Faith*, p. 34.

18. Dallin H. Oaks, *Pure in Heart* (Salt Lake City: Bookcraft, 1988), p. 63.

19. Bruce R. McConkie, *Doctrinal New Testament Commentary*, 3 vols. (Salt Lake City: Bookcraft, 1965–73), 2:159–160. See also Alvin R. Dyer, *The Meaning of Truth*, pp. 33–36.

20. Harold B. Lee, in Conference Report, October 1973, p. 7.

21. David O. McKay, *Home Memories of President David O. McKay*, compiled by Llewelyn R. McKay (Salt Lake City: Deseret Book Co., 1956), pp. 228–230.

22. Alvin R. Dyer, *The Meaning of Truth*, pp. 23–24.

23. First Presidency statement, February 15, 1978, as quoted in Spencer J. Palmer, *The Expanding Church* (Salt Lake City: Deseret Book Co., 1978), p. v.

24. Erastus Snow, in *Journal of Discourses*, 23:186–187.

25. Wilford Woodruff, "Our Lineage," *Topical Outline to the Way to Perfection*, (Salt Lake City: Genealogical Society of Utah, 1932), p. 4.

26. Joseph Fielding Smith, in *Church News*, July 10, 1971, p. 14.

27. Harold B. Lee, *Youth and the Church* (Salt Lake City: Deseret Book Co., 1970), p. 169.

28. Ezra Taft Benson, "In His Steps," *Speeches of the Year* (Provo, Utah: Brigham Young University Press, 1980), pp. 59–60.

29. Bruce R. McConkie, *A New Witness for the Articles of Faith*, p. 35.

30. Harold B. Lee, in Conference Report, October 1973, p. 7.

31. Brigham Young, in *Journal of Discourses*, 7:289–290.

32. Bruce R. McConkie, "God Foreordains His Prophets and His People," *Ensign*, May 1974, p. 72.

33. John Taylor, "The Origin and Destiny of Woman," in *The Mormon*, as cited in N. B. Lundwall, compiler, *The Vision* (Salt Lake City: Bookcraft, n.d.), pp. 145–148.

34. Joseph Fielding Smith, *The Way to Perfection* (Salt Lake City: Deseret Book Co., 1972), p. 44.

35. The First Presidency, 1971, as cited in Steve F. Gilliland, "I Have a Question," *Ensign*, June 1977, p. 40.

36. Joseph Fielding Smith, *The Way to Perfection*, pp. 44–45. Elder Boyd K. Packer also cautioned against the idea of a "predestined love" in an address entitled "Eternal Love" given at the BYU Tri-Stake Fireside, November 3, 1963.

37. Joseph Smith, *History of the Church* (Salt Lake City: Deseret Book Co., 1967), 6:364.

38. Wilford Woodruff, in *Journal of Discourses*, 18:114.

39. John Taylor, in *Journal of Discourses*, 23:177.

40. Wilford Woodruff, in *Journal of Discourses*, 22:334–335.

41. Neal A. Maxwell, in Conference Report, October 1985, p. 21.

42. Spencer W. Kimball, *The Teachings of Spencer W. Kimball*, edited by Edward L. Kimball (Salt Lake City: Bookcraft, 1982), pp. 315–316.

43. Joseph F. Smith, *Gospel Doctrine* (Salt Lake City: Deseret Book Co., 1939), p. 31.

44. See Bruce R. McConkie, "God Foreordains His Prophets and His People," *Ensign*, May 1974, p. 73. In a speech delivered in 1877, President Wilford Woodruff spoke of the signers of the Declaration of Independence and "fifty other eminent men" who had been raised up by the Lord for their missions. For a complete description of his vision of these men and an account of the temple ordinances completed in their behalf, see *Journal of Discourses*, 19:229.

45. M. Russell Ballard, in *Church News*, March 8, 1980, p. 4.

46. Bruce R. McConkie, *Ensign*, May 1974, p. 73.

47. Neal A. Maxwell, *Speeches of the Year*, 1978, p. 152.

48. See Harold B. Lee, "Understanding Who We Are Brings Self-Respect," *Ensign*, January 1974, p. 5.

49. Neal A. Maxwell, in Conference Report, October 1985, p. 21.

50. Wilford Woodruff, in *Journal of Discourses*, 22:334–335.

51. M. Russell Ballard, "You—the Leaders in 1988," *Ensign*, March 1979, pp. 71–73.

8

"Trailing Clouds of Glory"

Elder Bruce R. McConkie, speaking to religious educators at Brigham Young University, taught, "We just don't realize how much of everything we have in this life is based on pre-existence."[1] We have already seen how the doctrine of fore-ordination is related to the diversity among spirits in the pre-mortal world and how foreordination subsequently affects many aspects of our situation and experience in life. In ad-dition to foreordination to lineages, nations, families, and earthly missions, it appears from the inspired statements of modern prophets that the premortal life affects our lives in many other ways. We may not even be able to discern all of the effects of that previous life, but we can recognize at least some of the impact that experience has on our lives here. Wordsworth alluded to this thought when he poetically penned that we come into this world "not in entire forget-fulness,/And not in utter nakedness,/But trailing clouds of glory do we come/From God." Our trailing clouds of glory are those attitudes and aptitudes which we bring with us from afar and which influence and shape our lives here on earth. As one LDS scholar observed, "It might be said that we come to earth with a type of spiritual 'luggage,' having to a large extent packed our own bags."[2] Packed in the "premortal baggage" we bring to earth are individual capacities and characteristics, likes and dislikes, and dispositions and desires. However, all this spiritual luggage we take on our trip through mortality is shrouded by a veil of forgetfulness.

The Veil of Forgetfulness

Each of us comes into this life without a recollection of our former home. There may be several reasons why God imposed this memory block on all of us as we enter mortality, but for now we do not fully understand his reasons. The scriptures offer no explanation. Some significant statements, however, appear in sermons of some of the latter-day seers. By their seeric gift to perceive hidden truths, these prophets assist us in discerning more clearly the role of the veil in our mortal sojourn. President George Q. Cannon taught:

> It is not as it was before. We were then in the presence of God. Now there is a veil between us and our Father, and we are left to ourselves, to a certain extent. We are left to be governed by the influences that we invite, and there are any number of evil influences around us, whispering into our ears and hearts all manner of things. . . .
>
> It is a part of the plan of salvation, I say, connected with man's existence upon the earth that God should thus withdraw Himself, as it were, from man and that a veil should be drawn between Himself and man and that if knowledge of Him be obtained, it should be obtained by the exercise of great faith and continued labor on the part of His children.[3]

Elder Neal A. Maxwell has further explained how the veil of forgetfulness is a merciful gift from our loving Father in Heaven, drawn over our minds for our benefit and development.

> We define the veil as the border between mortality and eternity; it is also a film of forgetting which covers the memories of earlier experiences. . . .

There are poignant and frequent reminders of the veil, adding to our sense of being close but still outside. . . .

But mercifully the veil is there. It is fixed by the wisdom of God for our good. It is no use being impatient with the Lord over that reality, for it is clearly a condition to which we agreed so long ago. . . . Without the veil, we would lose that precious insulation which would constantly interfere with our mortal probation and maturation. Without the veil, our brief mortal walk in a darkening world would lose its meaning—for one would scarcely carry the flashlight of faith at noonday and in the presence of the Light of the World. Without the veil, we could not experience the gospel of work and the sweat of our brow. If we had the security of having already entered into God's rest, certain things would be unneeded. . . .

Fortunately, the veil keeps the first, second, and third estates separate—hence our sense of separateness. The veil avoids having things "compound in one" to our everlasting detriment (2 Nephi 2:11). We are cocooned, as it were, in order that we might truly choose. Once, long ago, we chose to come to this very setting where we could choose. It was an irrevocable choice. And the veil is the guarantor that our ancient choice will be honored.[4]

Elder Orson Pratt also taught that the "veil" was a necessary part of our mortal probation. He taught that even Jesus' premortal knowledge was veiled that he might be "left, as it were, in the very depth of humility, beginning at the very first principles of knowledge and growing up from grace to grace, as the Scriptures say, from one degree to another, until he received a fullness from his Father." Elder Pratt then applied this same principle to our own situation in life.

Now if his knowledge was forgotten, and his judgment taken away, why not ours? We find this to be the case. What person among all the human family can comprehend what took place in his first existence? No one, it is blotted from the memory, and I think there is great wisdom manifested in withholding the knowledge of our previous existence. Why? Because we could not, if we had all our pre-existent knowledge accompanying us into this world, show to our Father in the heavens and to the heavenly host that we would be in all things obedient; in other words, we could not be tried as the Lord designs to try us here in this state of existence, to qualify us for a higher state hereafter. In order to try the children of men, there must be a degree of knowledge withheld from them, for it would be no temptation to them if they could understand from the beginning the consequences of their acts, and the nature and results of this and that temptation. But in order that we may prove ourselves before the heavens obedient and faithful in all things, we have to begin at the very first principles of knowledge, and be tried from knowledge to knowledge and from grace to grace, until, like our elder brother, we finally overcome and triumph over all our imperfections, and receive with him the same glory that he inherits, which glory he had before the world was.[5]

As was the case with Jesus, it may also be with us that the more we grow in grace through righteousness and increased spirituality, the more the veil thins and the greater our understanding of the premortal world becomes. The Prophet Joseph Smith taught that "the nearer man approaches perfection, the clearer are his views."[6] Perhaps we will not regain all of the knowledge we possessed in the premortal world until we receive a fulness in the Father's kingdom. We can, however, recapture some of our forgotten premortal understanding through following in the footsteps of Christ, the Great Exemplar. President Joseph F. Smith explained:

> I believe that our Savior is the ever-living example to all flesh in all these things. . . .
> . . . He is our example. The works he did, we are commanded to do. . . . If Christ knew beforehand, so did we. But in coming here, we forgot all, that our agency might be free indeed, to choose good or evil, that we might merit the reward of our own choice and conduct. But by the power of the Spirit, in the redemption of Christ, through obedience, we often catch a spark from the awakened memories of the immortal soul, which lights up our whole being as with the glory of our former home.[7]

"This inner serenity," stated Elder Neal A. Maxwell, "which the believer knows as he brushes against the veil is cousin to certitude. The peace it brings surpasses our understanding and certainly our capacity to explain. . . . Even when the veil is parted briefly, it will be on His terms, not ours."[8]

There are those who are *in* the world and *of* the world who may use their lack of remembrance of our premortal home as evidence that we had no such existence. To those who would deny a premortal life simply because they cannot remember it, the following words resound. "The vail is thick between us and the country whence we came," declared Elder Orson Hyde. "We cannot see clearly—we cannot clearly comprehend—we have forgotten! . . . But our forgetfulness cannot alter the facts."[9]

Talents and Aptitudes

We have learned from modern revelation that "whatever principle of intelligence we attain unto in his life, it will rise with us in the resurrection. And if a person gains more knowledge and intelligence in this life through his diligence and obedience than another, he will have so much the advantage in the world to come." (D&C 130:18–19.) There are two dimensions to this concept—premortal to mortal and mortal to postmortal. This principle also applies to talents and aptitudes that spirits in the premortal world acquired through their "diligence and obedience" there. They bring with them to mortality these aptitudes in much the same way as we will take our intelligence and knowledge with us "in the world to come." Elder Bruce R. McConkie explained the application of this principle to the premortal world in this manner:

> Being subject to law, and having their agency, all the spirits of men, while yet in the Eternal Presence, developed aptitudes, talents, capacities, and abilities of every sort, kind,

and degree. During the long expanse of life which then was, an infinite variety of talents and abilities came into being. As the ages rolled, no two spirits remained alike. Mozart became a musician; Einstein centered his interest in mathematics; Michelangelo turned his attention to painting. . . .

The Lord endowed us all with agency; he gave us laws that would enable us to advance and progress and become like him; and he counseled and exhorted us to pursue the course leading to glory and exaltation. He himself was the embodiment and personification of all good things. Every desirable characteristic and trait dwelt in him in its eternal fulness. All of his obedient children started to become like him in one way or another. There was as great a variety and degree of talent and ability among us there as there is among us here. Some excelled in one way, others in another. . . .

. . . When we pass from preexistence to mortality, we bring with us the traits and talents there developed. True we forget what went before because we are here being tested, but the capacities and abilities that then were ours are yet resident within us. Mozart is still a musician; Einstein retains his mathematical abilities; Michelangelo his artistic talent; Abraham, Moses, and the prophets their spiritual talents and abilities. . . . And all men with their infinitely varied talents and personalities pick up the course of progression where they left it off when they left the heavenly realms.[10]

These previously acquired talents and abilities are evident in many ways here on earth. Mozart was an accomplished musician and composer at an age when other children are still playing with building blocks. In addition to child prodigies such as Mozart, there are often people who seem to have special inclinations that enable them to develop talents and skills more readily than others. We usually refer to them as "gifted" people or "naturals." It appears that the mortal manifestation of their abilities is enhanced by some previous experience. President Joseph Fielding Smith made this important statement in response to the question, "Why are some spirits born into the world with more ability than others?":

The spirits of men were created with different dispositions and likes and talents. Some evidently were mechanically inclined, from them have come our inventors. Some loved music and hence they have become great musicians. We evidently brought to this world some if not all of the inclinations and talents that we had there. The fact that one person finds one bent, like mathematics easy and another finds it difficult, may, in my judgment, be traced to the spirit existence. So with other talents and skills. . . . It is my judgment that thousands of others were chosen for their special fields because they showed talents and dispositions in that spirit world.[11]

Sometimes we see dramatic evidence of premortal talents and aptitudes emerging in the most interesting and often inexplicable ways. Several years ago the CBS News program *60 Minutes* presented a segment dealing with a unique psychological phenomenon known as the "autistic-savant syndrome." People with this condition possess extraordinary intellectual or artistic abilities even though they are severely mentally retarded. Often the feats performed by an autistic-savant surpass those of the most brilliant of "normal" people. Scientists are puzzled by this phenomenon and find the achievements of such individuals so remarkable that they defy belief and explanation. In the *60 Minutes* program three men with this condition were highlighted. One was an artist who produced remarkably beautiful and intricately detailed sculptures of horses; the second possessed unusual intellectual skills demonstrated by his complex mathematical skill and his incredible memory. The third, Leslie Lemke, was a most gifted musician with a unique story of his own. In a touching article entitled "The Miracle of May Lemke's Love," Joseph P. Blank has recounted the remarkable story of Leslie Lemke.

The Milwaukee County General Hospital had a serious problem: a six-month-old infant named Leslie. Mentally retarded and without eyes, the baby also had cerebral palsy.

He was a limp vegetable, totally unresponsive to sound or touch. His parents had abandoned him.

The hospital staff didn't know what to do—until a pediatrician mentioned May Lemke, a nurse-governess living nearby. A nurse telephoned May and explained that in all likelihood Leslie would die in a short time. "Would you help us by taking care of him while he lives?" the nurse asked.

"If I take him he certainly will not die, and I will take him," May replied. . . .

When May accepted the baby, she accepted him as just that, a baby—no different from others—to be taught and loved. . . .

She bathed him, cuddled him for hours, talked to him, sang to him. He never moved or uttered a sound.

Year after year she cared for him, but there was no movement. No smile. No tears. No sound. If May had not tied him to the back of the chair he would have toppled over.

May never stopped talking to him. She massaged his back, legs, arms and fingers. She prayed, and sometimes when she prayed she wept and put Leslie's hands to her cheeks so he could feel the tears. "I feel sad right now and I'm crying," she would say.

May refused to consider the child a burden. *I did not seek Leslie, so there has to be a reason why I was picked to raise this child,* she told herself. *God, in his time, will show me the reason.*

May was never reluctant to bring Leslie out in public. He was her boy, her love. She intuitively felt that somewhere in the maze of his damaged brain he was trying, and she was proud of him. . . .

. . . May took Leslie to a rehabilitation center in Milwaukee. No one thought anything could be done for the boy. There was not a single word of encouragement.

This professional pessimism didn't deter her. She *knew* that someday Leslie was going to break out of his prison. She just had to help him. She tried to think of a way to get the concept of walking into his mind. He had never made a move to crawl. He had never seen anyone walk.

... Taking steps, [May] would clasp Leslie's hands to her hips in the hope that he would absorb the walking motion. He just slumped and dangled behind her.

The Lemkes then had a chain-link fence erected along the side of their property, and May stood Leslie next to it, thrusting his fingers through the openings. After several weeks he finally got the idea of letting the fence support him. He stood. He was 16.

Then May tried to get him to move along the fence. She never stopped talking to him, encouraging him: "Come on, love, move just a little bit, a little bit." She said this hundreds of times, moving his hands and feet herself. Finally, he moved on his own. . . .

It was an interminable, grueling struggle, but May never thought of it as a struggle; she was simply striving to help her boy. . . . *Please do something for Leslie,* May prayed time and again. *He may be 18 years old, but he's still a baby. . . .*

One day she noticed Leslie's index finger moving against a taut piece of string around a package, as if plucking it. *Was this a sign?* she wondered. *What did it mean?*

Music! she exclaimed to herself. *That's it. Music.* From then on the Lemke house was filled with music. . . . Hour after hour the music played. Leslie gave no indication that he was listening.

May and Joe bought an old upright piano for $250 and placed it in Leslie's bedroom. Repeatedly, May pushed his fingers against the keys to show him that his fingers could make sound. He remained totally indifferent.

It happened in the winter of 1971. May was awakened by the sound of music. It was 3 a.m. Someone was playing Tchaikovsky's Piano Concerto No. 1. She shook Joe. "Did you leave the radio on?" she asked.

"No," he said.

"Then where's the music coming from?" She swung out of bed and turned on a living-room light. It dimly illuminated Leslie's room. Leslie was at the piano. May saw a smile glowing on his face.

He had never before got out of bed on his own. He had never seated himself at the piano. He had never voluntarily or deliberately struck the keys with his fingers. Now he was actually playing a concerto—and with deftness and confidence.

. . . Why the music burst out of him on that early-morning hour in late winter is unknown. But come it did, like a gale. His repertoire ranged through the classics, rock, ragtime, country-western and gospel.

. . . Leslie's skill at the piano steadily increased. His rendition of Gershwin's "Rhapsody in Blue" is a tour de force, flawless and evocative.

And he sings. Before learning to speak clearly he could readily mimic a variety of singers. He has a big, round voice and, when he pulls out all the stops, it can be heard a block away. He can do Luciano Pavarotti in two Italian operas, Jimmy Durante in "Inka Dinka Doo," Louis Armstrong in "Hello, Dolly!" and both parts of the Jeanette MacDonald–Nelson Eddy duet in "Sweethearts." . . .

As news of Leslie's talent traveled, groups requested him for concerts. . . .

Leslie played at churches, civic clubs and schools, and for groups of cerebral-palsy and retarded children and their parents. He went on to college, county fairs, local television and finally network television.

He loves performing. Sometimes he will burst into song while sitting in an airport lounge or airliner. People around him are often startled by his first notes, but his closing always is met with exclamations and applause.

There still are many things that Leslie cannot do. Those fingers that perform so brilliantly at the keyboard cannot use a knife or fork. Conversation does not flow easily. But ask what music means to him and he replies with a voice that is firm. "Music," says Leslie, "is love."[12]

(Excerpted with permission from the October 1982 *Reader's Digest*. Copyright © 1982 by The Reader's Digest Assn., Inc.)

Because of our knowledge of the premortal existence, we can perhaps understand better why there is so much diversity in talent, skill, and intellectual aptitude among the people of the world. This doctrine helps us to see more clearly the actual truth of the statement that someone is a "born" artist, musician, teacher, or possessor of other talents or abilities. It may also reveal the literal nature of the description "wise beyond one's years." It must be remembered, however, that although we may come into mortality with specific talents and aptitudes packed in our spiritual luggage, and although some things in life may come easier by virtue of our premortal accomplishments, those capacities must be nurtured and cultivated in this life, as well, in order to fully blossom. President Spencer W. Kimball stressed that we must not neglect those talents and abilities with which we came into the world.

> . . . God has endowed us with talents and time, with latent abilities and with opportunities to use and develop them in his service. He therefore expects much of us, his privileged children. . . .
>
> The great calamity, as I see it, is when you or I with so much potential grow very little. That is the calamity—when I could be so much and I am so little; when I am satisfied with mediocrity . . . in whatever I am going to do with my life; when I am satisfied with this, oh, that is a sad, sad day because it has an everlasting and eternal influence upon me.[13]
>
> Let us get our instruments tightly strung and our melodies sweetly sung. Let us not die with our music still in us. Let us rather use this precious mortal probation to move confidently and gloriously upward toward eternal life which God our Father gives to those who keep his commandments.[14]

As President Kimball so eloquently expressed, the Lord expects a great deal from us. We cannot be slothful in developing those skills which may be latent in our spirits, and we must also be diligent in acquiring new talents and aptitudes as well. Not having acquired certain capacities in the premortal life certainly does not preclude us from gaining them here. Indeed, that is part of the reason for our venture into mortality. Since some talents and abilities are not as readily apparent as others, there are those who may think that they did not come into this world with premortally developed abilities or that they have no capacity to develop any. It may not be immediately obvious which talents we packed in our spiritual luggage, but we must be diligent nonetheless, for as the Prophet Joseph taught, "All the spirits that God ever sent into this world are susceptible of enlargement."[15] The Lord also revealed to the Prophet "that every man may improve upon his talent, that every man may gain other talents, yea, even an hundred fold" (D&C 82:18). Therefore, we cannot neglect the fact that the Lord charged *all* spirits coming into mortality to "seek . . . earnestly the best gifts, always remembering for what they are given; . . . they are given for the benefit of those who love me and keep all my commandments, and him that seeketh so to do; that all may be benefited" (D&C 46:8–9).

Dispositions and Desires

The Book of Mormon prophet Amulek counseled us not to procrastinate repentance, "for that same spirit which doth possess your bodies at the time that ye go out of this life, that same spirit will have power to possess your body in that eternal world" (Alma 34:34). Just as the attitudes and inclinations we acquire in mortality follow us into the spirit world at death, it makes sense that propensities, dispositions, preferences, and even personality traits, to an extent, come with us into mortality from our premortal home. President Joseph Fielding Smith affirmed this idea when he said:

> Notwithstanding this fact that our recollection of former things was taken away, the character of our lives in the spirit world has much to do with our disposition, desires and mentality here in mortal life. *The spirit influences the body to a great extent, just as the body in its desires and cravings has an influence on the spirit.* . . . Environment and many other causes, however, have great influence on the progress and

destiny of man, but we must not lose sight of the fact that the characteristics of the spirit, which were developed through many ages of a former existence, play a very important part in our progression through mortal life.[16]

As President Smith pointed out, other factors such as environment and heredity influence our lives. It is interesting, however, to observe great differences even among people who share the same genetics and environment, as is often the case within families. It is not uncommon for parents to observe vast differences in personality, attitude, ambition, and many other traits among their children. Each is unique, even though he or she may have much in common with the rest of the family. One child may have tendencies to be rebellious or lazy, whereas another may be hardworking and obedient. One may be extremely outgoing and vivacious, and another shy, reserved, or even withdrawn. Even identical twins often exhibit stark differences in personal attributes. Such differences among children often cause parents to wonder, "How can each child be so different when raised by the same parents, in the same home?" No doubt there are many answers to this question. One major reason, however, is the pre-earth development of dispositions and desires that follow children into mortality like "trailing clouds of glory."

There are still other ways that our premortal inclinations may influence our lives here. A somewhat common way is discussed in the following correspondence between Elder Orson F. Whitney and President Joseph F. Smith.

Elder Whitney asked:

> Why are we drawn to certain persons, and they to us, as if we had always known each other? Is it a fact that we always have? Is there something, after all, in that much abused term "affinity" and is this the basis of its claim? At all events, it is just as logical to look back upon fond associations, as it is to look forward to them. We believe that ties formed in this life, will be continued in the life to come; then why not believe that . . . some of them at least, have been resumed in this state of existence?

President Smith responded to Elder Whitney's inquiry:

I heartily endorse your sentiments respecting congeniality of spirits. Our knowledge of persons and things before we came here, combined with the divinity awakened within our souls through obedience to the Gospel powerfully affects, in my opinion, all our likes and dislikes, and guides our preferences in the course of this life, provided we give careful heed to the admonition of the Spirit.

All those salient truths which come so forcibly to the head and heart seem but the awakening of the memories of the spirit. Can we know anything here that we did not know before we came? Are not the means of knowledge in the first estate equal to those of this? I think that the spirit, before and after this probation, possesses greater facilities, aye, manifold greater, for the acquisition of knowledge, than while manacled and shut up in the prison house of mortality.[17]

So powerful are those predilections acquired in the premortal realm, pointed out President Joseph F. Smith, that even likes and dislikes here in mortality, including our affinity for certain people, are affected. These "memories of the spirit" influence our lives and attitudes here on earth like echoes from eternity. Speaking of an experience of this type, President George Q. Cannon referred to these spirit memories and gave an example of what some may call *déjà vu.*

I was a boy when my people gathered with the Saints of God. I was very curious to know the Prophet Joseph, having heard a great deal about him. I happened to be in a large crowd of people where the Prophet was, and I selected him out of that large body of people. There were no means of recognition that I know of which would suggest him to me as the Prophet; but I recognized him as though I had always known him. I am satisfied that I had known him and been familiar with him. There are instances which all of us doubtless have known which have proved to us that there has been a spiritual acquaintance existing between us. We frequently say, "How familiar that person's face is to me." In this way kindred spirits are brought together. We are drawn together by this knowledge and this acquaintanceship which, I have no doubt, was formed anterior to our birth in this state of existence.[18]

There are surely countless other ways in which our acquisitions from the premortal life have bearing on our mortal lives. In most cases, we probably don't recognize them. Yet, as our lives unfold and as we live righteously so that we may begin to know who we truly are, we begin to understand that although there is a testing veil drawn between our first and second estates, it is only a veil and not a wall. Though our memories of that place may be held back, the "principles we attained unto" were packed in our bags and sent with us to earth. If we thoughtfully examine our lives and our inner selves, we will be amazed to discover that many, if not most, of our talents, aptitudes, dispositions, and desires trace their source to our previous existence. Besides recognizing these things in general, many of us would realize other specific situations unique to us as individuals. We not only are what we are—but, to a large extent, we are what we were. As Elder Bruce R. McConkie said, "We just don't realize how much of everything we have in this life is based on preexistence."

Notes

1. Bruce R. McConkie, "Preexistence of Man," unpublished lecture transcript of Summer 1967 Seminary and Institute Teacher Seminar, Brigham Young University, copy in author's file. Audiotape of lecture is available in the BYU Religious Education Audiovisual Library.

2. Larry E. Dahl, "The Preexistence," an unpublished paper in the possession of the author, Brigham Young University, 1987, p. 2.

3. George Q. Cannon, *Gospel Truth*, 2 vols., edited by Jerreld L. Newquist (Salt Lake City: Deseret Book Co., 1974), 1:7–8.

4. Neal A. Maxwell, "Patience," *Speeches of the Year* (Provo, Utah: Brigham Young University, 1979), pp. 219–220. Devotional address delivered at Brigham Young University, November 27, 1979.

5. Orson Pratt, in *Journal of Discourses*, 15:245.

6. Joseph Smith, *Teachings of the Prophet Joseph Smith* (Salt Lake City: Deseret Book Co., 1972), p. 51.

7. Joseph F. Smith, *Gospel Doctrine*, 17th edition (Salt Lake City: Deseret Book Co., 1971), pp. 13–14.

8. Neal A. Maxwell, "Patience," *Speeches of the Year*, p. 219.

9. Orson Hyde, in *Journal of Discourses*, 7:315.

10. Bruce R. McConkie, *Mortal Messiah*, 4 vols. (Salt Lake City: Deseret Book Co., 1979–1981), 1:23, 25.

11. Joseph Fielding Smith, *Answers to Gospel Questions*, 5 vols. (Salt Lake City: Deseret Book Co., 5th ed., 1972), 5:138–139.

12. Joseph P. Blank, "The Miracle of May Lemke's Love," *Reader's Digest*, October 1982, pp. 81–86. This story can also be seen on 16mm film and video, "May's Miracle," produced by Filmmaker's Library, Inc., New York City, 1981; and it is available from the producers and through BYU Media Services.

13. Spencer W. Kimball, *The Teachings of Spencer W. Kimball*, edited by Edward L. Kimball (Salt Lake City: Bookcraft, 1982), pp. 149, 173.

14. Spencer W. Kimball, as quoted in JoAnn Ottley, "A Musical Stewardship—Teacher of Life," *A Woman's Choices* (Salt Lake City: Deseret Book Co., 1984), p. 97; as quoted in Wilma Gardner, "Finding Joy in the Savior's Plan," *Ensign*, March 1988, p. 73.

15. Joseph Smith, *The Words of Joseph Smith*, edited by Andrew F. Ehat and Lyndon W. Cook (Provo, Utah: Religious Studies Center, Brigham Young University, 1980), p. 360.

16. Joseph Fielding Smith, *Doctrines of Salvation*, 3 vols. (Salt Lake City: Bookcraft, 1954), 1:60.

17. Orson F. Whitney and Joseph F. Smith, as quoted in Joseph Fielding Smith, *The Way to Perfection* (Salt Lake City: Deseret Book Co., 1972), pp. 45–46. See also Joseph F. Smith, *Gospel Doctrine* (Salt Lake City: Deseret Book Co., 1939), pp. 12–13.

18. George Q. Cannon, in *Deseret Weekly* (Salt Lake City, April 7, 1889), 38:676–677; cited also in George Q. Cannon, *Gospel Truth*, 1:4.

9

"Of Him Unto Whom Much Is Given Much Is Required"

The restoration of the true doctrines of the gospel of Jesus Christ was a gradual process rather than a single event. The Prophet Joseph Smith received inspired information "line upon line" from time to time. Upon receiving one such revelation, recorded in the Book of Moses, Joseph gratefully acknowledged that "amid all the trials and tribulations we had to wade through, the Lord, who well knew our infantile and delicate situation, vouchsafed for us a supply of strength, and granted us 'line upon line of knowledge—here a little and there a little,' of which the following was a precious morsel."[1] It could also be said that the restoration of the doctrine of man's premortal existence came to Joseph "line upon line . . . here a little and there a little." We come to a more acute awareness of the import and impact of this doctrine in our own lives in a like manner. It is to us, today, a most "precious morsel" of truth given to us by a loving Father to be, as Joseph declared, "a supply of strength." While our knowledge and understanding of the premortal life is incomplete, it will continue to expand as other "precious morsels" of the doctrine are unfolded before us. Even from the limited knowledge that we now possess come blessings of insight and inspiration and an enrichment of our earthly experience. We must remember, however, that with such blessings also come important opportunities and weighty responsibilities. The Lord has reminded us, "For of him unto whom much is given much is required" (D&C 82:3).

Blessings

One of the great blessings accompanying the knowledge of the premortal realm and our very real relationship to God is the perspective that we gain regarding the challenges of this life. Without this knowledge it would appear that God is arbitrary or even cruel. But with the restored truth of the premortal life, we can, as Elder Boyd K. Packer stated, "yield to the discipline of a loving Father and accept even the very hard lessons of life."[2] The enhanced understanding of our premortal experience not only expands our view of the eternal future and eternal past but also gives us a clearer vision of why we are here on earth. "We can cope with what seem to be very dark days and difficult developments," explained Elder Neal A. Maxwell. "We will have a true perspective about 'things as they really are,' and we can see in them a great chance to contribute." When this doctrine is "properly understood and humbly pursued," continued Elder Maxwell, it "can help us immensely in coping with the vicissitudes of life."[3]

The blessings associated with this knowledge are more than merely enlarged perspective. The Father also compassionately reminds us of our roots to encourage and motivate us. As we face the tasks and trials of mortality, we may sometimes feel downtrodden and discouraged, our reservoirs of spiritual strength depleted. It is at these crucial moments that our understanding of the role of premortal existence in our lives can become an ardent ally. This profound doctrine encourages, inspires, and motivates us to greater heights. It is, as Elder Neal A. Maxwell described, "a flash from the mirror of memory that beckons us forward toward a far horizon."

> When in situations of stress we wonder if there is any more in us to give, we can be comforted to know that God, who knows our capacity perfectly, placed us here to succeed. No one was foreordained to fail or to be wicked. When we have been weighed and found wanting, let us remember that we were measured before and we were found equal to our tasks; and therefore, let us continue, but with a more determined discipleship. When we feel overwhelmed, let us recall the assurance that God will not overprogram us; he will not press upon us more than we can bear (D&C 50:40).
>
> The doctrine of foreordination [and premortal life], therefore, is not a doctrine of repose; it is a doctrine for the second-milers; it can draw out of us the last full measure of devotion. . . .
>
> Yet, though [this] is a difficult doctrine, it has been given to us by the living God, through living prophets, for a purpose. It can actually increase our understanding of how crucial this mortal estate is and it can encourage us in further good works. This precious doctrine can also help us to go the second mile because we are doubly called.[4]

Another actuating aspect of these revealed truths is our grasp of the fundamental fact that we have power and potential to become like our Father in Heaven. This is no idle cliché or figurative phrase. Some worldly scoffers find this idea silly, others view it as heresy; but surely it is because they do not understand their own origins. This doctrine joyfully declares that we are literal children of God—we are of his royal lineage—we are heirs to a throne. "We are the children of God," declared President George Q. Cannon, "and as His children there is no attribute we ascribe to Him that we do not possess. . . . We existed with Him . . . as His children. . . . There is not one of us that He has not cared for and caressed. There is not one of us that He has not desired to save and that he has not devised [the] means to save."[5] Because we know from whence we came, we also know why we are here on earth, where we are heading, and what we must do with our time in this mortal sphere. Millions of God's children are groping in spiritual darkness in a quest for this same understanding. The privilege of having this knowledge and its accompanying blessings, when so many struggle through life without such guidance, places weighty responsibilities upon our shoulders.

Responsibilities

"Premortality is not a relaxing doctrine," proclaimed Elder Maxwell. "For each of us, there are choices to be made, incessant and difficult chores to be done, ironies and adversities to be experienced, time to be well spent, talents and gifts to be well employed."[6] When it comes to the responsibilities toward God and our fellowmen that are placed upon us by this doctrine, there can be no repose or relenting. Because of the blessings we enjoy by virtue of our knowledge of the premortal life, numerous opportunities for significant service to our Father in Heaven and to our spirit brothers and sisters await us.

Our Responsibilities to Our Heavenly Father

Elder Bruce R. McConkie reminded us that "a knowledge of these wondrous truths places upon us a greater burden than rests upon any other people to follow Christ—to take his yoke upon us, to keep his commandments, to do ever those things that please him. And if we love and serve him, we will give heed to the words of the apostles and prophets whom he sends to reveal and teach his word among us."[7] Our desire to do whatever is required of us to return to God's presence should be intensified by our innate feelings of homesickness and our enhanced understanding of what our heavenly home *was* and *will yet be*. The scriptures soberly caution, however, that "he who sins against the greater light shall receive the greater condemnation" (D&C 82:3). President George Albert Smith emphasized this message when he stated:

> [God] has given us intelligence and wisdom above our fellow men. A knowledge of pre-existence has been given to the Latter-day Saints [Sec. 49:17; 93:23, 29]; a knowledge that we are here because we kept our first estate, and that we have been given the opportunity of gaining eternal life in the presence of our heavenly Father, by keeping our second estate. [Abraham 3:22–26.] We will not be judged as our brothers and sisters of the world are judged, but according to the greater opportunities placed in our keeping. We will be among those who have received the word of the Lord, who have heard His sayings, and if we do them it will be to us eternal life, but if we fail condemnation will result.[8]

The Lord has given us a "precious morsel" in the doctrine of premortal life to bless our lives and to guide us in the fulfillment of our highest destiny. We cannot ignore or reject the impelling implications of that truth. In this the second estate, we can neither be smug in this special knowledge nor complacent in our commitment to the cause of Christ. Elder James E. Talmage penned, "Man is untrue to his divine lineage and birthright . . . when he turns away from the truth, or deliberately chooses to walk in darkness while the illuminated path is open to his tread."[9]

Our Responsibilities to Our Fellowmen

King Benjamin plainly taught that our charge to serve God is intimately intertwined with our responsibilities toward our fellowmen. "I tell you these things that ye may learn wisdom; that ye may learn that when ye are in the service of your fellow beings ye are only in the service of your

God" (Mosiah 2:17). The Savior, likewise, declared that there are two commandments, upon which "hang all the law and the prophets"—*love God* and *love thy neighbor* (see Matthew 22:37–40). As the knowledge and spiritual understanding of our premortal existence intensifies our love for our Father in heaven and his Son, Jesus Christ, and increases our determination to serve them and keep their commandments, so should the sense of service and commitment to compassion likewise swell within our souls. John the Beloved taught that we cannot keep the first great commandment without also keeping the second.

> If a man say, I love God, and hateth his brother, he is a liar: for he that loveth not his brother whom he hath seen, how can he love God whom he hath not seen?
> And this commandment have we from him, That he who loveth God love his brother also. (1 John 4:20–21.)

We who understand the literal nature of the brotherhood of humanity possess a greater obligation to serve others. By virtue of our baptismal covenants and our knowledge of how each of us is truly related, we recognize that we cannot love and serve God and neglect our responsibilities to others. Alma taught us that our covenant with God includes a promise to, first, "stand as a witness of God at all times and in all things, and in all places," and, second, be "willing to bear one another's burdens . . . mourn with those that mourn . . . comfort those that stand in need of comfort" (see Mosiah 18:8–9). Elder John A. Widtsoe taught that, in addition to our mortal covenants, we made premortal covenants that committed us to the Father's work and glory—"to bring to pass the immortality and eternal life of man" (Moses 1:39).

> In our preexistent state, in the day of the great council, we made a certain agreement with the Almighty. The Lord proposed a plan, conceived by him. We accepted it. Since the plan is intended for all men, we became parties to the salvation of every person under that plan. We agreed, right

then and there, to be not only saviors for ourselves but measurably, saviors for the whole human family. We went into a partnership with the lord. The working out of the plan became not merely the Father's work, and the Savior's work, but also our work.[10]

Service to Our Fellowmen
Through Missionary Efforts

Our lives are blessed by the knowledge that has come to us through the restoration of the gospel of Jesus Christ. The insight and inspiration that we have enjoyed regarding our premortal life with God adds to the abundant life which Christ has promised (see John 10:10). As valuable as this knowledge is to us, we cannot selfishly keep it to ourselves or we will lose the blessings associated with that knowledge. "The eternal truth is," wrote President Thomas S. Monson, "that which we willingly share, we keep; and that which we selfishly keep to ourselves, we lose."[11] While we bask in the inspired illumination of the restored truths of the gospel, "there are many yet on the earth among all sects, parties, and denominations, who are blinded by the subtle craftiness of men . . . , who are only kept from the truth because they know not where to find it" (D&C 123:12). Because we have come to greater light and truth—specifically the truth of who we are and from whence we came—a greater obligation rests upon us to "waste and wear out our lives in bringing to light all the hidden things of darkness" (D&C 123:13). Elder Hyrum M. Smith, a member of the Quorum of the Twelve and son of President Joseph F. Smith, implored the members of the Church:

> You Latter-day Saints ought to praise God; but in your thankfulness for the greater blessings which you enjoy, you ought not to denounce others because they have not so much good as you have. No; our whole souls should be filled with pity because of their condition, and we should

sympathize with them because of their ignorance and blindness because they are being led by blind guides. We should go forth among them with the sole desire of our hearts to manifest unto them that which God has revealed unto us, and carry to them that which has made us happy, and which has made us in very deed the Church and people of God. That should be the feeling of the Latter-day Saints.[12]

Not only should we boldly and unwearyingly proclaim the gospel message to all of our spirit siblings, whom we knew and loved premortally, but also our lives should reflect the profound truths contained in the simple phrase, "I am a child of God." The doctrine of premortal life and the universal brotherhood of man places upon us a responsibility to share these truths with others by both precept and example. President Harold B. Lee, in his last general conference address, petitioned us to conform our personal lives to the divine image of God inherent in each of us so that we can have greater influence on others.

I would charge you to say again and again to yourselves . . . "I am a [son or a daughter] of God" and by so doing, begin today to live closer to those ideals which will make your life happier and more fruitful because of an awakened realization of who you are.

God grant that each of us here today may so live that all among us, and with us, may see, not us, but that which is divine and comes from God. With that vision of what those who have lost their way may become, my prayer is that they may receive strength and resolution to climb higher and higher and upward and onward to that great goal of eternal life and also that I may do my part in seeking to show by example, as well as by precept, that which will be the best of which I am capable of doing.[13]

Strengthening Our Fellowmen
Through Compassionate Service

If the veil of forgetfulness were lifted from our minds temporarily so that we could remember who our former friends and dearest companions were in the premortal world, we undoubtedly would view the needs of our earthly fellowmen in sharper perspective. We would more clearly recognize our neighbors, acquaintances, and even our enemies, as members of our own spirit family. As Latter-day Saints, however, we should not need to have the veil lifted, because we already know by revelation that we are, in truth, brothers and sisters to every inhabitant of the earth. With this knowledge, the Savior's words "Inasmuch as ye have done it unto one of the least of these my brethren, ye have done it unto me" (Matthew 25:40) take on a more literal, rather than merely symbolic, meaning. Now we, of all people, should recognize that our actions toward others have impact on the entire family of God. Our enlarged understanding of the premortal world gives richer meaning to the inspired words of John the Beloved.

> Hereby perceive we the love of God, because he laid down his life for us: and we ought to lay down our lives for the brethren.
> But whoso hath this world's good, and seeth his brother have need, and shutteth up his bowels of compassion from him, how dwelleth the love of God in him?
> My little children, *let us not love in word, neither in tongue; but in deed and in truth.*
> Beloved, let us love one another: for love is of God; and every one that loveth is born of God, and knoweth God.
> He that loveth not knoweth not God; for God is love. . . .
> . . . If God so loved us, we ought also to love one another. (1 John 3:16–18; 4:7–8, 11; italics added.)

While the rest of the world speaks of love for fellowman in the context of a simply symbolic view of "universal brotherhood," we have the awesome obligation, by virtue of our vision of the literal relationship of humanity, to "succor the weak, lift up the hands which hang down, and strengthen the feeble knees" (D&C 81:5). "The more we serve our fellowmen in appropriate ways, the more substance there is to our souls," wrote President Spencer W. Kimball. "We become more significant individuals as we serve others. We become more substantive as we serve others—indeed, it is easier to 'find' ourselves because there is so much more of us to find!"[14]

The doctrine of premortal life, of our being children of God, can stimulate us toward a more significant sense of service and spirituality, which, if acted upon, enlarges our souls and our sense and testimony of who we really are. Our foreordinations provide opportunities to serve in mortality, not just rewards and recognition for premortal achievement. As we strive to keep our second estate and prove faithful here as we were there, we must continually search for our spiritual roots, finding ourselves and gaining that understanding of our true identity that comes only through keeping *both* of the great commandments. Elder Neal A. Maxwell, noting that "it has only been in recent times—since people started saying they loved mankind—that neighbors have suffered so much neglect," went on to admonish:

> So often what parched and thirsty people need is to be nourished by drinking of deep doctrines and to be revived by the food of fellowship. Giving genuine companionship to the malnourished mortals who have known so little love and so few friends is as vital as food for the starving.
>
> So often we can serve by bathing the wounded and bruised egos of others in the warm waters of deserved commendation.
>
> So often what people need is to be enveloped in the raiment of real response.
>
> So often what people need so much is to be sheltered from the storms of life in the sanctuary of belonging. Such a service cannot be rendered by a selfish people, however, because the response of the selfish will always be there is no room in their inn.
>
> You and I are believers, and preachers of a glorious gospel which can deepen all human relationship now as well as projecting all relationships into eternity. . . .

We, more than others, should not only carry jumper and tow cables in our cars but in our hearts by which means we can send the needed boost or charge of encouragement or the added momentum to mortal neighbors. . . . Service keeps us from forgetting the Lord our God, because being among and serving our brothers and sisters reminds us that Father is ever there and is pleased when we serve, for while the recipients of our service are our neighbors—they are His children.[15]

No, the doctrine of premortal life is not a relaxing doctrine. It not only serves to reassure us but also unremittingly reminds us of responsibilities to our Heavenly Father and to each of our spirit siblings. It is a doctrine of perspiration as well as inspiration—a doctrine of required actions as well as renewed acquaintances. As we strive and struggle with the challenges of the second estate, we may often feel overwhelmed and even discouraged. As difficult as our journey through life may seem, that "secret something" that whispers to our souls, "You're a stranger here," also whispers mercifully, "You are not alone." We must hearken to those inklings of immortality and remember that this is where we chose to be—the premortal prospects of which shook the heavens with resounding shouts of joy. As President Ezra Taft Benson reminds us:

A few years ago, we knew our Elder Brother and our Father in Heaven well. We rejoiced at the upcoming opportunity for earth life that could make it possible for us to have a fullness of joy like they had. We could hardly wait to demonstrate to our Father and our Brother, the Lord, how much we loved them and how we would be obedient to them in spite of the earthly opposition of the evil one.

And now we're here—our memories are veiled—and we're showing God and ourselves what we can do. And nothing is going to startle us more when we pass through the veil to the other side than to realize how well we know our Father and how familiar his face is to us. And then, as President Brigham Young said, we're going to wonder why we were so stupid in the flesh.

God loves us. He's watching us, he wants us to succeed, and we'll know someday that he has not left one thing undone for the eternal welfare of each of us. If we only knew it, there are heavenly hosts pulling for us—friends in heaven that we can't remember now, who yearn for our victory. This is our day to show what we can do—what life and sacrifice we can daily, hourly, instantly bring to God. If we give our all, we will get his all from the greatest of all.[16]

Notes

1. Joseph Smith, *History of the Church* (Salt Lake City: Deseret Book Co., 1967), 1:98.

2. Boyd K. Packer, in Conference Report, October 1984, pp. 82–83.

3. Neal A. Maxwell, "Meeting the Challenges of the Day," *Speeches of the Year,* (Provo, Utah: Brigham Young University, 1978), p. 155.

4. Neal A. Maxwell, *Speeches of the Year,* 1978, p. 156, 151.

5. George Q. Cannon, *Gospel Truth,* 2 vols., edited by Jerreld L. Newquist (Salt Lake City: Deseret Book Co., 1974), 1:1–2; as quoted in Carolyn J. Rasmus, "Happiness the Lord's Way," *Ensign,* March 1988, p. 47.

6. Neal A. Maxwell, in Conference Report, October 1985, p. 21.

7. Bruce R. McConkie, "God Foreordains His Prophets and His People," *Ensign,* May 1974, p. 73.

8. George Albert Smith, in Conference Report, October 1906, p. 47, as cited in Roy W. Doxey, comp., *Latter-day Prophets and the Doctrine and Covenants,* 4 vols. (Salt Lake City: Deseret Book Co., 1978), 3:44.

9. James E. Talmage, *The Vitality of Mormonism,* pp. 280–282, as quoted in Roy W. Doxey, *Latter-day Prophets and the Doctrine and Covenants,* 4 vols. (Salt Lake City: Deseret Book Company, 1978), 3:45–46.

10. John A. Widtsoe, "The Worth of Souls," *Utah Genealogical and Historical Magazine*, October 1934, pp. 189–190.

11. Thomas S. Monson, "Status Report on Missionary Work," *Ensign*, October 1977, p. 11.

12. Hyrum M. Smith, in Conference Report, October 1903, pp. 70–71.

13. Harold B. Lee, in Conference Report, October 1973, p. 10.

14. Spencer W. Kimball, "Small Acts of Service," *Ensign*, December 1974, pp. 2, 5.

15. Neal A. Maxwell, "When the Heat of the Sun Cometh," unpublished address delivered at Young Adult fireside, Salt Lake Tabernacle, May 20, 1979; transcript of this talk in the possession of the author.

16. Ezra Taft Benson, "Insights: We Seek That Which Is Praiseworthy," *Ensign*, July 1975, pp. 62–63.

Index